FAITH UNDER ATTACK

Learn How to Overcome Your Delays, Disappointments and Failures

written by
Lawrence Mukoro

SUTTON, ALASKA

Visit our website at **www.relevantpublishers.com**

Copyright © 2021, Lawrence E. Mukoro
Copyright © 2021, Relevant Publishers LLC, Cover design

All Rights Reserved. No part of this publication may be reproduced, stored in a retrieval system or transmitted in any or by any means, electronic, mechanical, photocopy, recording or any other, except for brief quotations in printed reviews, without the prior permission of the author.

Scripture quotations taken from the Amplified® Bible (AMP), Copyright © 2015 by The Lockman Foundation. Used by permission. www.lockman.org

Scripture quotations marked (NLT) are taken from the Holy Bible, New Living Translation, copyright ©1996, 2004, 2015 by Tyndale House Foundation. Used by permission of Tyndale House Publishers, Carol Stream, Illinois 60188. All rights reserved.

Scripture quotations marked (CEV) are from the Contemporary English Version Copyright © 1991, 1992, 1995 by American Bible Society, Used by Permission.

Scripture quotations marked (MSG) are taken from THE MESSAGE, copyright © 1993, 2002, 2018 by Eugene H. Peterson. Used by permission of NavPress, represented by Tyndale House Publishers. All rights reserved.

Scripture quotations from The Authorized (King James) Version marked (KJV). Rights in the Authorized Version in the United Kingdom are vested in the Crown. Reproduced by permission of the Crown's patentee, Cambridge University Press

Relevant Publishers LLC
PO Box 505
Sutton, AK 99674

Faith Under Attack, Learn How to Overcome Your Delays, Disappointments, and Failures/ Mukoro, Lawrence E. - North American Edition

ISBN: 9781953263056 ebook
ISBN: 9781953263049 print book

DEDICATION

I dedicate this book to my sweet and gorgeous wife
Lily Mukoro
As my teammate, you have been with me through many unbearable delays, disappointments and failures. Together we have come out of them all on the other side victoriously. Honestly, I admire the grace of God upon your life, and I am so proud to be your husband.
I love you!

CONTENTS

ABOUT THE BOOK I
INTRODUCTION II

CHAPTER 1 1
FAITH UNDER ATTACK 1
- Understanding The Attack 2
- What Is Faith? 4
- Why Is Faith Being Attacked? 5
- Accessing Your Strength 6
- Contend For Your Faith 8
- Who Is Behind The Attack? 10
- Attacks Are Not Alien 12
- Violation of the Second Commandment 14

CHAPTER 2 17
FAITH DOESN'T WALK ALONE 17
- The Dangers of Walking Alone 18
- God's Timing 19
- God's Promises Don't Manifest Overnight 20
- Patience The Stabilizer 22
- Failure Before Success 23
- Personal Wounds 26
- Fundamental Doctrines 27
- The Early Church vs Today's Church 28

CHAPTER 3 30
PATIENCE 30
- The Impatient Servant 32
- The Prodigal Son 34
- The Strong Will Faint 35
- Who Appoints the Time? 38
- The Death of Lazarus 39
- God Waits For Us 41

CHAPTER 4 43
DECEPTIVE PATIENCE. 43

- Waiting and Complaining 45
- Waiting But Not Ready 46
- The Foolish Virgins 48
- Waiting in Hopelessness 50
- Waiting in Fear. 50
- Waiting Without Joy. 52
- Waiting Without Prayer. 53
- The Early Days of Our School 54
- Waiting In Disobedience 56
- The Great Marriage 58

CHAPTER 5 61
MOTIVATIONS 61

- God's Goodness 64
- God's Faithfulness. 66
- God's Wisdom. 68
- Our Love For God. 69
- My Encounter 70

CHAPTER 6 72
THE TRIMESTERS OF PATIENCE 72

- Who Is The Helper?. 74
- Developing Patience. 74
- The Word Trimester. 75
- The Heart Trimester. 76
- The Hope Trimester. 76
- Trial and Delivery 77
- The Example of Jesus Christ 79

CHAPTER 7 82
7 LIES WE CANNOT BELIEVE. 82

- We Won't Be Able To Enjoy It 84
- Others Are Getting Ahead 85
- People Are Laughing 87
- It Will Never End 88
- It Isn't Worth It. 89

    God's Timing Is Wrong 90
    Patience Is Weak and Powerless 91

CHAPTER 8 93
DEALING WITH DISAPPOINTMENTS 93

    Letting Go 94
    Beauty For Ashes 96
    Starting Over. 97
    The Hidden Blessings 98

CHAPTER 9 100
DISCERNING THE SEASONS 100

    Discernment: A Gift. 102
    A Word In Season 103
    Growing Up 104
    Nehemiah Discerns The Season 106
    Paul's Second Missionary Journey. 108
    Man-Made Delays & Failures 110
    Maximizing The Seasons 111

CHAPTER 10 113
WHY PRAY? 113

    Prayer Creates and Maintains an Intimate Relationship With God . 113
    Prayer is a Sign of our Dependency and Reliability on God 114
    Prayer is an Invitation to God to Intervene in our Circumstance . . 114

CHAPTER 11 116
7 IRRESISTIBLE PRAYERS. 116

    Stand in Righteousness When You Pray 116
    Pray With Expectation and Faith 117
    Be Specific When you Pray. 118
    Pray According to God's Will 120
    Pray with Humility 121
    Be Persistent When You Pray. 122
    Pray with Praise 124
    Rest, Wait, and See 125

CHAPTER 12 128
GOD'S PAY DAY. 128

Why Does God Keep His People Waiting? 129
Doors Will Open On Their Own 131
God's Fast Lane 132
The Glory Will Dwarf The Suffering. 133
Justice For Your Enemies 134
God Will Give You A New Song 136

EPILOUGE 137
People Just Like You 137
ABOUT THE AUTHOR 139
PRAYER OF SALVATION 140
LAWRENCE MUKORO MINISTRIES 141

About The Book

Faith under attack is simply faith under test, faith under pressure, or faith against oppositions that come to us in the form of delays, disappointments and failures. These are often offensive and unbearable attacks we shall all face as Christians. The enemy is using them as traps to shake our faith, that is, to make us doubt God's love and care.

Yet, rejoice because we aren't helpless. God is on our side. He wants to help us by using these same attacks to add a stabilizer to our faith that will keep us undisturbed, unperturbed and ultimately prevent us from giving up in the face of the unbearable. While we are patient, God is working to bring us out of the situation completely.

The Bible says, God causes all things to work together for the good of His people. Are you presently going through a season of delay, disappointment, or failure? If yes, then this book, Faith Under Attack, is just for you! The Biblical truths and insights embedded inside this book will help you experience peace of mind, spiritual growth and victory in your season of delay, disappointment and failure. WOW! Bet, you don't want to miss this book.

Introduction

About three years ago, I received a message from one of the friends and partners of our ministry, who once served as the team lead in our medical missions at the early days of our ministry's evangelistic work. At first, I was pretty disturbed by her message until I took it to the Lord in prayer. Read it for yourself:

"I have prayed, fasted and by His grace I'm walking in obedience to God- I don't live in pride, I give to the needy, pay my tithe. What else haven't I done? I have been asking the Lord for other things and He gives them to me but why is this particular one still delaying? Maybe, I don't know how to pray about it. Please, can you teach me how to pray about my marital life?"

Allow me to put my friend's message into a simple sentence. "I'm doing the will of God, but why am I still facing delay in getting married?" My friend was becoming troubled and doubting God's promises because her Mr. Right wasn't forthcoming. The situation was becoming unbearable for her. Well, the moment I finished reading her message I knew I couldn't offer her my opinion. It will be misleading and powerless. Really, she needed a specific word from God, a Rhema, which would require a specific response of her faith. So, I made up my mind not to reply to her message until I heard a word from the Lord.

Thankfully, this event occurred on a Saturday morning which gave me the awesome opportunity to do a prayer walk around our ministry building. Shortly after I started praying, I felt these words in my heart, "Tell My daughter to wait and keep trusting Me." Instantly, I wrestled with those words within me. I refused to accept it as an answer for my friend – I thought I was hearing myself.

Let's just say, I never thought those words were powerful enough to encourage her. However, I was totally wrong. The next word I heard proved my error and cleared my doubt. The Lord said again: "I never said the heroes of faith obtain their promises through faith alone (Hebrew 6: 12). So why can't you encourage My daughter to patiently trust Me as you share your own testimonies with her and those of other Christians who have also overcome?" To put it simply, "Tell her not to be troubled but to hold on and never give up." At this point, my doubt completely vanished, and God's peace filled my heart. That was the moment that inspired me to write this book. It was as though I was loaded to recharge not only her faith but also the faith of everyone facing similar conditions all over the world.

Immediately, after I received those words I went into our house to share them with my wife, Lily, before calling my friend. Amazingly, my friend was so encouraged and lifted after the Holy Spirit used me to plant those seeds of encouragement into her heart and her mood changed dramatically. That is what the truth of God's Word can do for you. It will set you free from whatever is holding you down. Well, before ending the call to my friend, I prayed for her.

It will amaze you to know that while I was writing this book recently, my friend phoned me to break the good news of her wedding bells. To the glory of the Lord Jesus, she is happily married today, and we are so excited because she has her victory at last.

Similarly, I know this is the fate of many Christians today. Perhaps you or someone dear to you is being troubled and feels like giving up on God's promises because of the delays, disappointments, or failures in your homes, relationships, finances, careers, health, ministry, having children, or some other area of life. The good news is, like my friend, you can overcome if only you will accept God's instruction to be patient. Don't be troubled, but hold on and never give up until your victory comes, because patience is the stabilizer your faith needs in moments of attack. This is what my book, Faith Under Attack, is all about. It will help you experience peace of mind, spiritual growth and victory in your waiting season if only you will wait patiently.

My hope is that as you read this book you will allow God's truths in it to strengthen and stabilize your faith until your own breakthrough comes. Remember Acts 10: 34 says, "God is no respecter of persons." That means what He did or does for someone, He's able to do for you too.

Join me, and let's get started!

Lawrence Mukoro

CHAPTER 1

FAITH UNDER ATTACK

I tell you, He will defend and protect and avenge them speedily. However, when the son of Man comes, will He find [persistence in] faith on the earth?
Luke 18:8 AMP

Most of the injustices done in many places in the world today are religious injustices, attacks against people of faith. The Christian faith is not an exception to this unfair treatment and experiences attacks even in countries with a rich Christian heritage and history. Simply, the church of Christ is facing strong oppositions and pressures both externally and internally.

Every day for a couple of hours, one of the ways my wife and I relax from daily tasks at our church and school is by sitting in our living room in the evening to watch and listen to sermons of Bible teachers we admire for their Christian fruits and witness. Also we watch both local and world news. On most occasions, these two daily activities leave us grieved, and they have given us opportunities to pray and intercede for believers all over the world as well. Sometimes, it's either a missionary who is being slaughtered or imprisoned, or a Christian community under physical attacks from gunmen, or young girls and women being abducted, or a child whose rights are taken away, or a person facing death because of their refusal to renounce Jesus Christ, or a political leader is facing social backlash for stirring his/her nation in a godly direction. The list goes on for those needing prayer.

When we see these sights, they sadden us so much because evil seems to be prevailing at the moment. On the other hand, we are glad, because we are seeing scriptures being fulfilled in our very eyes. This has in many ways strengthened our blessed hope and faith in Christ, that the end is near, and our King is coming soon to finally put an end to evil and the secret works of darkness. The prayer of the apostle John is now our prayer and should be the prayer of every believer during these troubling times. Jesus said, "Surely I come quickly," and John replied "Amen. Even so, come, Lord Jesus" (Revelation 22: 20).

The Bible and Church history has proven no attack whether spiritually, politically, or culturally orchestrated against the Church right from the first century until today has ever weakened the resolve, faith, growth or influence of the Body of Christ, known as the Church. The reasons are because the Church is born from above, and everything that is from above is above all (John 3:31). Jesus, the head of the Church, said, "...I will build my church; and the gates of hell shall not prevail against it" (Matthew 16:18). Also, the Church is the pillar and foundation of Truth (1Timothy 3:15), and the Truth will always prevail (2 Corinthians 13:8). Simply put, the Church is unstoppable!

But the enemy who is behind these attacks on the Church is a tireless destroyer, devourer and a trickster. He works in many ways and will stop at nothing to overthrow our faith. Another way the enemy is attacking is by indirectly stirring us up individually against God through the delays, disappointments, and/or failures we face in our everyday life. The enemy wants to cause Christians to doubt God's sovereign love and care for us.

UNDERSTANDING THE ATTACK

The attacks of delays, disappointments, and failures are very powerful. Sometimes they are unbearable, offensive and unavoidable. The enemy is either orchestrating them or using them as opportunities to deceive believers against God's sovereign love and care for us. Before we go further, we need to understand the meanings of these attacks: the 1828 *Webster Dictionary* defines "Delay" as: "to prolong the time of acting, or proceeding. Additionally delay means "to retard; to stop, detain or hinder for a time; to restrain motion, or render it slow." The New Strong Exhaustive Concordance of the Bible defines "Disappointment" as "the non-fulfillment of one's hopes." While the *Microsoft Encarta Dictionary* defines "Failure" as "lack of success in or at something."

From the above definitions, one can see that if a believer's hope is prolonged, hindered for a time, or appears to have failed at the moment, the result is disappointment. Disappointment creates feelings of unhappiness, worry, anxiety, and fear. These negative emotions are traps of the enemy to trouble the heart of God's people and cannot coexist with the Christian faith. Believers must quickly turn them over to the Lord, or else they will grow into complaints, compromise, and discouragements. Do you know that when God's people worry or complain, they are indirectly saying, God doesn't care for them, neither does He have control over things? Think about that for a moment!

Well, I want you to know that delays, disappointments, and failures are not actually the root cause of these negative attitudes towards God. They only enhance seeds of mistrust in God buried deep in a believer's heart. Delays, disappointments, and failure serve as a fan upon these small coals, which were thought to be quenched by salvation. However, when negative experiences happen, like fresh air rushing it, they breathe life on those old coals and produce a burning flame if we allow it. The revelation that believers still hold a place of mistrust in God is a beautiful gift of grace, because it allows us the opportunity to learn and trust Him more.

Have you ever seen Christians who face the pressure of delays, disappointments, or failures and handle it admirably without any alarm? One perfect example of handling trials is our Lord Jesus. In spite of all the troubles He experienced, He was not disturbed but maintains a deep peace within. So what is this scorching fire in us that happens to be the root cause of our worries, anxieties and fears? It's called IMPATIENCE. Period! Impatience is the mother of most ungodly actions and behaviors we see today in our homes, churches and societies. Stemming from selfishness, where the ego demands attention now, impatience influences our negative emotions, minds and actions. Our worries, anxieties, fears, complaints, compromises and discouragements are often fruits of impatience. They are developed from and strongly influenced by the impatience in our sinful nature. Until we understand and deal with our sinful old nature, we will continue to be trapped by these negative and ungodly attitudes just like the Israelites in the wilderness.

Thankfully, we are not helpless! God wants to help us, and He needs our cooperation to do so. God wants us to take advantage of our delays, disappointments, and failures by seeing them as opportunities to develop a stronger and more stable faith that can lead to a flourishing intimate relationship with Him and a victorious life through His help. In short, your attack today is a test for your promotion tomorrow. This is the reason God allows believers to go through trials and suffering. It's not because He doesn't care or lacks control over things. Instead, God uses Satan's attacks as a means to bless us. What you're going through right now is a blessing in disguise. I want you to think about that for a moment. When this revelation fully dawns on you, it will put you on the overcomer's side. Can you recall this book's cover picture again? It's a hand of water racing to quench or overcome a hand of fire, which is the impatience in us. If you keep reading, you will discover what the hand of water is. But before you go deeper, let me first shed light on what faith is, because believers need to understand Biblical faith to navigate the rest of this book without confusion.

What Is Faith?

Words are powerful, and they can transform our lives. However, the transformative power of a word begins with understanding the meaning of the word. So, what is faith? First, let's look up the dictionary meaning. According to *Vine's Dictionary of New Testament* the word "faith" is a "firm persuasion," a conviction based upon hearing and is used in the New Testament always to describe faith in God or Christ, or spiritual things.

But let's now come to the Bible and learn a more functional definition of faith. The writer of Hebrews wrote, "Now faith is the substance of this hope for, the evidence of things not seen" (Hebrews 11:1). The New Living Translation puts it this way, "What is faith? It's the confident assurance that what we hope for is going to happen. It is the evidence of things we cannot see."

Looking at all these definitions, let me simply sum it up: "Faith is a firm conviction or confidence in God and His Word." This means if someone has faith, he or she will strongly believe God exists and that everything His Word said about Jesus Christ is true, as well as everything else in the Bible, including God's promises. In other words, unless your conviction or trust is firm or confident in God's promises, it's considered as not active or functional faith.

Let's examine some synonyms for the word firm: stable, secure, fixed, steady, resolute, resolved, determined, concrete, and certain. Firm's antonyms include unstable and uncertain. Now, imagine a ship in a stable or calm river. The stability of the river will make the ship to be stable too. But when a storm or a boisterous wind comes upon the river, then the ship will wobble or be tossed about if it doesn't have a stabilizer or anchor. The same is true of a person's faith. If it is shaken or hit by a strong force, it can lose its firmness or confidence and begin to wobble, producing worry, anxiety and fear. It would be safe to say that in the troubles, faith became unstable. One major factor that can shake the firmness of the believer's faith is when a trial is intensified by delay, disappointment and/or failure. From these additional forces, doubt arises, and when a believer doubts God's promises, we are disconnected from the flow of God's power into our lives.

Allow me to put this into perspective, let's just say the things you hoped for are prolonged beyond your expected timeline or they appear to not manifest or lack the success you desired. Let me ask you, would your faith still remain firm or would you feel uncertain about receiving the thing you hoped? If you say your faith would stay firm, for how long would you continue to hope if the delay went on for years or even decades? A sincere answer will tell you why delay, disappointment, and failure are powerful weapons of the enemy against a believer's faith. It also explains why our faith needs a stabilizer: something to keep our hearts calm and established through troubling times to prevent us from giving up in the process. That stabilizer is PATIENCE (It's the hand of water racing to quench or overcome the hand of fire on this book's cover picture). Patience needs to walk side by side with faith so faith doesn't give up on its hopes. Before we discuss more on how patience is a helpmate to faith, let's first find out why faith is being attacked.

WHY IS FAITH BEING ATTACKED?

I have a friend who is a captain in the Nigerian Army. We have been buddies from college. After graduation, he joined the military while I got a job in the telecom industry as a site supervisor, even though my background is in geology.

It happened we met again in one of the cities in Northern Nigeria when I was still on my secular job, and he was on a military deployment at that time. He was a godly man, and outside of work, we were able to catch up and deepen our friendship.

From our conversations and my visits to the barracks, I took an interest to study some military books but not for the purpose of joining the army. I already knew from college I was called to preach Jesus Christ for the rest of my life. However, I'm a curious person from childhood, and one way I've found answers to my questions was through studying books. Now, I wanted to know about military leadership, wars, strategies, and so on. After time of studying military books and through our personal discussions, I gathered something about military strategy regarding an enemy attack. This tactic is a well-known battle strategy used in the Bible to gain victory over their enemy. This is it: To defeat an enemy conquer their strength by taking advantage of their weakness.

Simply, a man's weakness is an access to his strength. However, as Christians, we are the enemy of the enemy. Satan is always out to conquer our strength through our weaknesses. A believer's strength is his/her FAITH, a firm or confident trust in God and His Word. Faith is what the enemy desires to destroy, but he doesn't come directly at our faith because he knows through our faith we can resist and defeat him, so he takes advantage of our weaknesses. Listen to what Jesus told Peter before His crucifixion: "Simon, Simon, Satan has asked to have all of you, to sift you like wheat. But I have pleaded in prayer for you, Simon, that your FAITH should not fail. So when you have repented and turned to me again, strengthen and build up your brothers" (Luke 22:31-32 NLT).

Notice what Jesus prayed about for Peter. He prayed for Peter's faith, that it fail not. That quickly tells us two things: One, Peter's faith was the target of Satan's attack, and second Peter's faith was his strength. This is true for Christians today. Our faith is our strength, and it's the target of the enemy, not our relationships, finances, health, children, or whatever other means the enemy attacks. Those are our weaknesses, which Satan uses to get to us emotionally. Our faith is our real strength, without which we cannot prevail against the enemy nor can we connect to or receive from God. My functional definition of faith states: Faith is the supernatural power that enables us to connect to and receive from God. This definition will help you to see why doubt disconnects believers from the flow of God's power in their lives. Don't let the enemy access your weakness!

ACCESSING YOUR STRENGTH

Do you remember Samson, the great Jewish warrior who terrorized and terrified Israel's enemy in the Bible? For years the Philistines were helpless in the hands of Samson until they hired Delilah to find where his great strength lay: "And the lords of the Philistines came up to her and said to her, 'Entice him, and find out where his great strength lies, and by what means we may overpower him, that we may bind him to afflict him; and every one of us will give you eleven hundred pieces of silvers'" (Judges 16:5).

Notice Delilah was hired to find Samson's source of strength, not his weakness. The reason is because Delilah was already Samson's weakness. Samson was very loose with women. The previous verse tells us, "he (Samson) loved a woman in the Valley of Sorek, whose name was Delilah." She was the Philistines access to conquer Samson's great strength. We all have our weaknesses; Samson's was women or Delilah. The apostle Peter's weakness was his self-confidence. Mine was anger. What's yours? Is it unforgiveness, jealousy, pride, greed, addiction, pornography, alcohol or lying?

Do you get frustrated when things you desire are delayed? Do you want to surrender or give up when things are difficult or fail? Do you find it hard to let go of a person or situation when you've been mistreated or hurt? Whatever your weakness, don't resort to self-pity, self-condemnation, or guilt, because the same grace by which you are saved is the grace available to empower you through your weaknesses. Hear the Lord's reply to the apostle Paul when he prayed three times for the Lord to remove a thorn in his flesh, which Satan has brought on him: "And He (Jesus) said to me, "My grace is sufficient for you, for My strength is made perfect in weakness" (2 Corinthians 12:9).

Did you catch that? God's grace is all you need to be set free from your weakness, because the power of Christ is strong in our weakness. Stop weeping over your weaknesses, as if you are helpless. Instead, start appropriating the divine empowerment available to you through Christ right where you are. If you aren't sure how to do that, look at the rest of the passage: "Therefore most gladly I will rather boast in my infirmities, that the power of Christ may rest upon me."

The word infirmities means weakness or inability. Some translations use weakness instead of infirmities in this verse, like in the New Living Translation. Paul is simply saying, I will be glad in my inabilities and will not feel ashamed about them so that the power of Christ, that is, the ability of Christ can come on me in this area of my life.

Think about Samson. He was a strong man, but he was only strong so long as God's power was on him. Otherwise, he was like every other man. Do you recall when God's ability left Samson after the seven locks of his hair were shaved off his head, the Scriptures says: "...So he awoke from his sleep, and said, 'I will go out as before, at other times, and shake myself free!' But he did not know that the Lord had departed from him" (Judges 16:20).

In other words, you are weak in an area when you haven't given room to the power of God to rest there. I encourage you to turn your impatience and other weaknesses completely over to Jesus. You will be amazed how He will turn them into strength for you, and where you were weak before you will see new strength and victory arise.

CONTEND FOR YOUR FAITH

To contend means to strive or struggle to obtain, or to defend or preserve something, as two competitors contending for a prize that only one can win. Take it or leave it. We are in a contest with the devil over faith. There are many reasons for this battle:
- Ephesians 2:6 tells us by grace are we saved through faith.
- Romans 3:28 proclaims a man is justified by faith.
- James 1:6-7 says we receive God's promises through faith.
- Mark 11:22-24 explains with faith we can create miracles.
- 1 Peter 5:9 warns us we resist the devil through faith.
- Ephesians 6: 12 tells us we quench the flaming arrows of the wicked through faith.
- Galatians 3:11 states the just shall live by faith.
- 2 Corinthians 5:7 declares Christians walk by faith.
- Hebrews 11:6 tells us without faith nobody can please God.
- Romans 14:23 warns us whatever is not from faith is sin.

Simply summarized, faith is the strength, lifeline, and backbone of all believers. With faith a believer is unstoppable, more than a conqueror, and a victor not a victim. Faith makes us powerful. That's why the enemy is doing everything he can to ensure unbelievers never get faith and upset believers who have it to cause them to lose or mistrust it. Yet, this should give you reason to fight for your faith, even against seemingly insurmountable circumstances and especially in seasons of delay, disappointments, or failures.

Be determined and courageous to fight for your faith. Never give in to the pressure or opposition of the enemy. Difficult circumstances are a test and a process to refine your faith to make you stronger and a more stable believer. But when we are pressed beyond measure, how do we contend for our faith? Jude provides us with an answer: "Keep yourselves in the love of God" (Jude 21).

What is the love of God? God's love for us is unconditional and undeserved. We didn't do anything to earn it, and we can't do anything to lose God's love either. A deep understanding of God's love for you will change your life forever. It will also empower you to show love to Him in return and that help keep you in His unchanging and unfailing love in seasons of delays, disappointments, and failures. Paul the apostle tells us one way we can show love to anyone including God is through being patient: "Love is patient" (1 Corinthians 13:4 NLT).

When we patiently wait for God to work in our lives in the midst of troubling circumstances, we are demonstrating our love for God. This is why when Paul prayed for the Thessalonica Church, he said: "May the Lord direct your hearts into [realizing and showing] the love of God and into the steadfastness and patience of Christ and in waiting for His return" (2 Thessalonians 3:5AMP).

In other words, when you love God, you will be patient in the midst of hardship because patience is proof of love. Patience will stabilize your faith through dark times and prevent you from giving up. It's a stabilizer when added to your faith to keep you calm. Patience also stymies you from giving up in the middle of the process before your victory arrives.

Do you remember the story of Job? The devil wasn't really out for Job's children, health or wealth. Those were just a means for Satan to attack Job's firm trust or love for God. But boy, Satan barked up the wrong tree! Scriptures tell after all the attacks, Job retained his integrity toward God, even when his wife urged him to curse God and die (see Job 2:9-10). I think the saying "the downfall of a man is not the end of a man" was coined from the story of Job.

But how did Job contend or keep his faith in those dark moments of his life? Job had the faith stabilizer, patience. Job didn't just have faith; he had patience also. Hear what Job said in his difficult and trying times as he was being attacked directly by Satan: "For there is hope of a tree, if it be cut down, that it will sprout again, and that the tender branch thereof will not cease...all the days of my appointed time will I wait, until my change come" (Job 14:7, 14).

It takes a man of great patience to say and keep those words of faith: to keep believing somehow he would be restored and that he was willing to wait until the time came. Job's great hope in God's faithfulness is exemplified by his willingness to patiently wait for his blessings to appear again. Job's patience reflected his love for God. No wonder the apostle James encouraged early Christians to imitate the patience of Job in times of suffering and trials (James 5:7-11). I'm sure courage and determination is already arising within you right now to keep your faith until your change comes. But who are you really contending with? Who is behind your attacks?

WHO IS BEHIND THE ATTACK?

One way we can defend ourselves against attack is by knowing who our enemy truly is. Otherwise, believers end fighting the wrong person and lose the battle. Sadly, this is where many Christians miss the mark. They lose the battle even before the fight begins, because the real enemy is taking advantage of their ignorance. That is what the Prophet Hosea explained, "My people are destroyed for lack of knowledge…" (Hosea 4:6). And Jesus states it plain and clear: "And you will know the truth, and the truth will set you free" (John 8:32).

So what is the Truth about our enemy? The truth is the devil, Satan, Lucifer, or any other name you'd like to call him, as the Bible has many names for the enemy of our souls, is the real and common enemy of every Christian. If you are a believer, Satan is your enemy. Satan clearly sees Christians as his enemy too, because of our faith in Jesus Christ. Let's look up some scriptures that will convince you Satan is your enemy:

- "The thief (Satan) does not come except to steal, and to kill, and to destroy. I (Jesus) have come that they may have life, and that they may have it more abundantly" (John 10:10)
- "For though we walk in the flesh, we do not war according to the flesh" (2Corinthians 10:3)
- "For we do not wrestle against flesh and blood, but against principalities, against powers, against the rulers of the darkness of this age, against spiritual hosts of wickedness in the heavenly places" (Ephesians 6:12)
- Be sober, be vigilant; because your adversary the devil walks about like a roaring lion, seeking whom he may devour. (1 Peter 5:8)

Perhaps you've never fully understood Satan is your personal enemy. It makes you want to catch your breath for a moment! Oftentimes, believers see only the physical person with whom they may be dealing with as the enemy. But scripture makes it clear, Christians are not at war with other people. We are at war with a spiritual enemy who impacts the physical realm. It isn't your family, friends, colleagues, neighbors or those people on the other side that are after you. It is the devil! The person who hurt you, maltreated you, slandered you, mocked you, or persecuted you is not your real enemy. Perhaps you are saying in your heart, "Wait a minute Lawrence. That is not true. So and so is my enemy; he hurt me." Oh yes, what I'm saying is true! Those people who hurt you or did all kinds of evil to you and your family were used or hired by the devil.

Most people are totally unaware they are working for the devil. Just like Delilah was hired to take Samson down, many people are ignorantly working for Satan to take Christians down. Sadly, even some Christians are being used by the devil to hurt other Christians. Delilah wasn't Samson's real enemy, the Philistines were but they used her to get to him. Let me put it differently, the devil is masquerading through people around you. He's like a puppet master, pulling human strings to get people to act out against you. The people aren't your real enemy, Satan is.

Matthew 16:21-23 tells how Jesus was explaining to his disciples that He must go to Jerusalem, where he will suffer, die, and be raised after three days. Then Peter took Jesus aside and rebuked Him, saying such a thing will not happen. The passage tells us Jesus rebuked Satan, not Peter directly. Jesus knew the real enemy was Satan, not Peter. Satan was masquerading through Peter. Another incident in the Bible was when Peter denied Jesus three times during His trial. If you recall earlier Jesus had told Peter that Satan desired to take him out, but He (Jesus) had prayed for Peter to not give up when it happened. Do you know how Satan carried out his attack on Peter's faith? He used two men and a young woman to confront and intimidate Peter (see Luke 22:31-32, 56-60).

In my short walk with the Lord, I have seen believers who thought if they are not getting married, bearing children, getting their dream job or being promoted, then some family member or friend was responsible for their delay or disappointment. Worse, these believers felt they must find out spiritually who is behind their lack by identifying a physical person. This kind of mentality is not the gospel of Christ and only breeds hate among loved ones. The gospel of Jesus Christ is a gospel of love, not a gospel of hate as some people now portray it. As preachers, we have to do a lot of work to help believers to grow up in their faith and not raise a bunch of miracle seekers with no depth to their faith.

So believers need to settle once and for all who their enemy is. Your enemy is the devil and his demons. He may masquerade through people around you, but those people are not your enemy. Jesus, Stephen and the apostles knew this truth and that is why they were able to forgive, prayed for, and even blessed the people who persecuted them. Believers are called to imitate Christ. To do this, we must see as Jesus saw and understand spiritual truths as He understood, and that begins with knowing who your real enemy is. It also means knowing how much God loves you, just as God loved Christ. God is a God of justice, so trust He will repay everyone who has hurt or mistreated in His timing and in His measures not yours. Your job, like Christ, is to learn to overcome evil with good (Romans 12:17-21). By choosing to believe in God's good promises in the midst of evil, you will bring peace and healing to your wounded soul and help others on their journey of faith.

ATTACKS ARE NOT ALIEN

As a believer in Christ, we are soldiers of Christ. Therefore, we must think and act like soldiers, always cultivating the characteristics of a soldier. Some of the characteristics of a soldier are: they endure hardship or tough times; they don't entangle with civilian's business; and they are always armed to fight opposition. Soldiers are not alien to battles. We as Christians should exemplify this character too.

Let's look at some of Paul's last words written from jail while awaiting trial in Rome to encourage Timothy to be strong in God's grace against the pressure and opposition he was facing and would face in his evangelistic ministry. Paul writes: "You therefore must endure hardship as a good soldier of Jesus Christ. No one engaged in warfare entangles himself with the affairs of this life, that he may please him who enlisted him as a soldier" (2 Timothy 2:3-4).

In other words, Paul was saying, as a soldier you must be prepared to endure whatever comes to you all the way to the end if you want to please the Lord. That is, add endurance, perseverance, or patience to your faith if you want to finish well. This should not be new to anyone who thinks of himself as a soldier of Christ. Simply said, if a believer doesn't have patience, he can't finish well.

Next, let us look at Peter's words to believers in the five provinces of Asia Minor, at a time of intense persecution under the Roman Empire. In his first epistle Peter addressed a major theme–believers suffering in Christ, as a way to encourage them to have a good attitude so that they could overcome until the end. Let me just quickly highlight Peter's entire message.

Primarily, attacks or suffering are a test of faith and should be viewed as a precious process to refine our faith, and if we can endure through them, they lead to praise, honor, and glory for us at the end. Secondly, the prophets of old prophesied about the suffering of Christ. Our sufferings enable us to identify with Him and His sufferings, and when we overcome, we shall share in His glory. Additionally, we should endure suffering or persecution from people when it's unjustly inflicted upon us for the sake of Christ, the gospel, and His kingdom. Righteous suffering is commendable and acceptable by God. The Lord considers it a precious thing because as you are enduring wrongful suffering, you are displaying the love of God for the world, just as Christ did. The bible also makes it clear that it is better to suffer doing God's will and doing good than to suffer for doing evil or wrong. Suffering for righteousness has a great reward, just like Christ who suffered for our sins and is in glory in heaven.

Furthermore, Peter encouraged believers to be fortified and armed and prepared for suffering, because it is the process that matures our faith. Suffering or trials are not a strange or foreign thing. Instead, they are something we should embrace and rejoice over, because through them, we have been given an opportunity to be partakers of Christ's suffering. We are not the only ones experiencing suffering either. Believers all over the world are facing similar struggles and conquering by faith through them. Finally, Peter reminds us that our suffering is only for a while. The time of trouble will have an end. It is often said in Christian circles, "this too shall pass! When it passes then our glory begins." What a deep truth is held in this quote. I encourage you to read the entire letter of First Peter. It will encourage and recharge your faith against suffering and give you hope to endure and overcome.

Now allow me to state clearly here that one way we suffer for Christ righteously is when we endure delays, disappointments and failure we didn't create ourselves. This kind of suffering wasn't strange or alien to early Christians and shouldn't be to believers today either. However, if believers are ignorant of the purpose of suffering or delays, they won't be prepared to handle these disappointments when they come. Jesus assures believers in the world we will have trouble (John 16:33), but also says to be of good cheer because He has overcome the world. Understanding God has a good purpose for suffering can encourage believers. When you are evaluating your journey of faith, don't neglect the importance of patience. Patience is the stabilizer to faith when things are delayed or they appear to be failing. It is essential to have patience if you want to finish well. Patience will keep your emotions, minds and actions under complete control and help you deal with people and things you cannot tolerate.

VIOLATION OF THE SECOND COMMANDMENT

Shortly after the Israelites departed Egypt, precisely three months into their journey from Egypt, they came to the wilderness of Sinai. There they camp by the mount. It was at Mount Sinai they received the Ten Commandment. Prior to this, God asked Moses to sanctify His people, that is, let them take time to clean up and purify themselves. God wouldn't reveal Himself to unclean people. As promised after Israel's purification, God's presence manifested in a thick cloud upon the mountain with smoke, fire, thunder, lighting and an exceeding loud voice of trumpets upon the mount. Unfortunately, this caused Israel to tremble and quake greatly. In short, God's presence descended upon Mount Sinai in His power, glory and majesty and it was unlike anything the Israelites had ever seen before. Basically, you can say they were overwhelmed by God's presence.

And in the midst of these manifestations, God spoke with Moses on the mountain top while all the other people stayed down below, hearing as God gave the Ten Commandments verbally. The second commandment said, "Thou shall not make any graven image unto thyself." However, since God knows the significance of a written document, which serves as a witness between Him and His people in the future. He asked Moses to come closer and stay in the mount with Him while He wrote the Commandments on stone tablets. This is also true for the scriptures on scrolls and gathered together in the Bible like we have today. Also it could be a scroll or Bible for teaching His people like the one we have today. In regard to God's request that Moses come alone, Moses asked Aaron, Hur and the seventy elders who were with Him to return to the people at the camp. Aaron was deputized to fill in for Moses during the period he would be away with the LORD. Only Joshua stayed on the mount waiting for Moses, and it appears the LORD never had a problem with him waiting (see Exodus 19-24).

Now let us go to chapter 32 as I present the rest of the story in scriptural text: "Now when the people saw that Moses delayed coming down from the mountain, the people gathered together to Aaron, and said to him, "Come, make us gods that shall go before us; for as for this Moses, the man who brought us up out of the land of Egypt, we do not know what has become of him" (Exodus 32:1).

I have highlighted the phrase "the people saw that Moses delayed coming down" to unveil two profound lessons that will change your thinking. Allow me to break this phrase into two sections: which are "the people" and "Moses delayed coming down." The scripture says, "the people saw that Moses delayed... and the people gathered to Aaron and said to him, "Come, make us gods that shall go before us..."Now the question is who were "the people"? Were they the men, women, young men, young women or even the children in the camp? Come with me to the next verse as I unfold their identity: "And Aaron said to them (the people), "Break off the golden earrings which are in the ears of your wives, your sons, and your daughters, and bring them to me" (Exodus 32:2).

Did you catch that? These *"the people"* who asked Aaron to make them gods and as such violated the second Commandment God just gave them are NOT the women, young men, young women or the kids in the camp. Instead, they were the men, the leaders and the influencers of Israel, which included Hur, Nadab, Abihu and the seventy elders who encountered God at the mount and even saw His feet, ate, drank and enjoyed fellowship with Him (see Exodus 24:9-10). They were the people who received the laws from God and the same people who led Israel into idol worship and immorality, acts highly prohibited by God.

What does that tell you? The problems we face today in our homes, churches, and the global society are mainly caused and aggravated by the wrong choices that parents and leaders are making. Simply, our problems are ninety nine percent leadership problems. As a young leader, this sounds a strong warning to me personally.

But why did these men and leaders of Israel make this wrong decision? The answer is found in the second section of the phrase: Moses delayed coming down. The word delayed here is translated from the Hebrew word boosh, which means to be disappointed, ashamed, to be put to confusion or be long. These leaders became disappointed and confused because Moses stayed too long on the mountain in their opinion. The Bible reveals Moses stayed on the mountain for forty days, not forty weeks or forty months or even forty years. Forty days (1 month and 10 days). Let me ask you, do you think Moses overstayed his time on the mountain, or do you think Moses stayed too long that those leaders couldn't endure? More importantly, let's find God's thought on this. The answer is right in verse 8: "They have turned aside QUICKLY out of the way which I commanded them" (Exodus 32:8).

Notice the word QUICKLY. It literally means soon, rapidly, fast, speedily, swiftly, hurriedly, hastily, at once, instantly, suddenly, instantly, abruptly and briefly. It was God who said these words. This should tell us that, sometimes what we see as delay, God sees it as our impatience. Also David said about this event when recalling God's faithfulness to Israel all through their journey from Egypt: "They soon forgot His works; They did not wait for His counsel" (Psalm 106:13).

Now be honest with yourself, are those words above not a perfect description of IMPATIENCE? We discussed earlier that impatience influences the emotions, minds and actions of people. Can you see how impatience influenced the decision of Moses associates to make the wrong choice? These were people who earlier had met and ate, drank and enjoyed fellowship with God. Now they allowed their impatience to lead to the loss of many lives in the camp. I warned you, when you are walking the journey of faith, remember to carry patience; it is your stabilizer.

CHAPTER 2

FAITH DOESN'T WALK ALONE

That you do not become sluggish, but imitate those who through faith and patience inherit the promises.
Hebrews 6:12

Companionship is such a great gift God has given to mankind. Having someone to talk to, support you, comfort you, cheer you, trust you, pray with you, accompany you, walk or work with you in any moment of life is worth more than silver and gold. It's priceless! The Garden of Eden was a perfect world, breathtakingly paradise. It had it all: beauty, splendor, natural resources, awesome nature, wonderful creatures, and God's presence, but still Adam wasn't satisfied. Think about that for a moment. Then God Himself, not Adam, said: "it is not good that man should be alone." That is the power of companionship, partnership or a teammate. God designed a helpmate for Adam because God knew humans were created to live in fellowship, in community.

In short, companionship or partnership is a gift through which we can achieve more than when we are alone. Honestly, I'm so glad to have this gift in my wife, Lily. I can't imagine being without her. Since we got married, aside the love and togetherness we share as a couple, we have achieved more together in our family life and ministry through the grace of God than if either of us were to be alone trying to accomplish the same goals. Many couples, partners and friends working together can attest for this truth. This is why King Solomon says: "Two are better than one. Because they have a good reward for their labor" (Ecclesiastes 4:9).

Similarly, faith and patience are better as a couple; they act as partners and friends when employed together and can achieve far greater things than if either of them walked or worked alone. The Christian walk is a marathon not a sprint. It is a long-distance race, not a short jaunt. It requires a lot of patience or endurance and fortitude to overcome the obstacles we encounter on our way to the finish line: the place where the promises will be received.

Conversely, when we run without patience, the stabilizer of faith, our faith becomes weak, and we can be discouraged when the race gets long or tough, desiring to give up before reaching the finish line. That is why the writer of Hebrews encouraged us to run with patience: "And let us run with patience the race that is set before us" (Hebrews 12:1 KJV). But what is wrong when our faith tries to endure the race without its partner, patience?

THE DANGERS OF WALKING ALONE

Walking alone shouldn't be encouraged at any time. Here is why: "For if they fall, one will lift up his companion. But woe to him who is alone when he falls, for he has no one to help him up" Ecclesiastes 4:10. Do you hear that? "WOE TO HIM WHO IS ALONE!" We all need someone to help us up when we fall because falling either physically or symbolically is a condition that happens to everyone. Do you remember the story of Samson? He was an exceptional and powerful judge in ancient Israel who ruled in the midst of his enemies. One of my favorite parts of his story is when the Philistines heard one day that he was in town, lodging with a harlot for the night. They quickly rally up together, put up watchmen, and lock the city gate to prevent him from going out until they can get their hands on him. Yet, at midnight when Samson was done with the harlot, he came out and found the city gate locked. Guess what he did? Samson pulled up the gate on his shoulder and went through it. Truly, he was a terror to Israel's enemy. Sadly, he was also a lone star; he had no teammate, at least none who sincerely had his best interests at heart. As a result, Samson ended up as a victim.

The same can be true for faith as well. Faith is an exceptional, powerful force in the universe with which we can terrorize the enemy, pull away every gate, break free from traps, and make our enemies watch helplessly as we rule in their midst like Samson. But, if we lack patience, as our stabilizer, then we lack the power that faith needs to hold it up when under severe pressure or facing strong opposition.

God's Timing

Faith and patience are partners that walk and work together. Faith needs patience as an essential companion because God has a right time for doing things. Yet, faith alone cannot wait for God's timing. Take a look at these words: "For ye have need of patience, that, after ye have done the will of God, you might receive the promise" (Hebrews 10:36 KJV).

In other words, between where you are and where the promise is, there is a chasm needing a bridge called patience. Patience enables us to wait for God's right time to manifest. Sadly, many Christians fail to receive their reward not because they didn't do the will of God, but because they lacked patience to wait and gave up before the promise arrived. Think about my friend in the beginning of the book whose story I shared in the introduction. According to her message, "I have done the will of God, but still my Mr. Right hasn't come." Then when she obeyed the Lord by being patient, her promise manifested. Maybe, like my friend, you have truly done the will of God but your promise isn't in view yet, and you don't know what else to do. I know what else you should do. You need to have patience my friend.

But what exactly is patience? Patience comes from two Greek words, Hupo meaning "under" and mones meaning "remain." Therefore, patience is the ability to remain "under pressure without complaining." Now let's look at an English definition. The Longman Dictionary of Contemporary English defines patience as "the ability to continue waiting or doing something for a long time without becoming angry or anxious. Or is the ability to accept trouble and other people's annoying behavior without complaining or becoming angry." Patience is translated in the Bible at times as endurance, perseverance, longsuffering and steadfastness.

From the above definitions, we can understand patience means endurance, perseverance, forbearance, longsuffering and steadfastness. These are the various aspects of Biblical patience, and they are what this book unveils. When a patient person faces delays, disappointments from people or failure in their life pursuit, they won't complain or become worried, anxious and angry. Instead, they learn and glean experience from the situation.

Sadly, the opposite is true for an impatient person, proving worry, anxiety, and fear are fruits of impatience, not our circumstances. If these negative traits are not addressed quickly, they will lead to complaining, compromise, and discouragement. This is because both impatience and patience influence our emotions, minds and actions. How we respond to people and circumstances prove whether we are patient or impatient.

GOD'S PROMISES DON'T MANIFEST OVERNIGHT

Patience is very important, because God's promise doesn't manifest overnight. See this truth illustrated in the life of Abraham. At seventy-five years, Abraham was married to Sarah but childless. Then God called him out of his country and away from most of his family into an unknown land where God would give to him and his children for an inheritance. Straightaway, Abram obeyed God and left with everything he had, including his wife, Sarah, and his nephew, Lot.

Years went by and Abraham was blessed materially, but he was still childless and had not yet taken full control of his promised land. Then one day, God appeared to him in a vision reassuring Abram of His protection. God also encouraged Abram to not be afraid after he defeated the kings that abducted his nephew, Lot.

Abram responded by reminding God he was still childless, which meant he had no heir to continue his legacy. Abram suggested to the Lord he would adopt one of the young men born in his house to become his heir. This practice took place in ancient cultures which was dominated by slaves and servants. However, God rejected the idea and stated explicitly Abram would father his own child. It must be noted when God spoke in Genesis 15 to Abram, He was speaking of Isaac, who would be born of Sarah, Abrams' barren wife. The Bible says Abraham believed God's words, and God counted it for him as righteousness (See Genesis 15:1 – 6).

Abraham's life lesson should teach us that we don't always have the right solution to our problems. At first Abraham was considering his servant for an heir to solve his own problems, but God had a better plan. God always does. As their conversation closed, the LORD reaffirmed to Abraham he would still inherit the land of Canaan, and Abraham desiring to know how this would happen asked God for a sign. To that end, God told him to prepare a sacrifice that will enable God to enter a covenant with Abram. After Abraham did, God spoke to him. One thing God said will not sit well with most Christians today: "Then He said to Abram: 'Know certainly that your descendants will be strangers in a land that is not theirs, and will serve them, and they will afflict them four hundred years'" (Genesis 15:13).

Does that sound like a pleasant prophecy to receive? I want you to know that the frightening thing in the above scripture is not that Abraham's children will be a stranger in a foreign nation, neither is it because they would be servants there, or the fact that another nation would afflict them. No, the most frightening aspect is, they would be there for four hundred years.

You may probably be thinking, "Lawrence, you think being a slave in a foreign nation and suffering hardship and torment from a foreigner oppressor is not a big deal? Oh yes, it is! But let me explain my position by asking you a simple question? Would you consider being a servant for a day or forty days in foreign nation with a lot of hardship and unfair treatments as a costly price to pay in exchange for owning your own beautiful country filled with vast natural resources? Of course not; nearly everybody would rush at that opportunity. However, this was not going to be the case with Abraham descendants. They would be in slavery for four hundred years. Who wouldn't agitate at this thought for their children, grandchildren and great-grandchildren? Anytime I preach about Abraham's children being in captivity for four hundred years as a promise from a loving God, it never sits well with the congregation. Remember four hundred years is not forty years neither is it four days, and slavery hardly seems like a good promise for God to pronounce on his friend.

Take notice how God used the adverb word "certainly" in this verse. Other synonyms for the word are "surely, definitely, without doubt, undoubtedly, and unquestionably." In other words, God is saying, "Abraham I have made up my mind and you cannot change it or question me why" as opposed to God allowing Abraham to challenge His actions and intervene in chapter 18 when Abraham negotiated the salvation of Sodom and Gomorrah because of his nephew Lot. In this proclamation, God carved it in a stone, and nothing could change the final verdict. Do you know that even with this bad prediction, God granted Abraham mercy to not be alive to witness the manifestation of this awesome promise God gave him, The LORD added: "Now as for you, you shall go to your fathers in peace; you shall be buried at a good old age" Genesis 15:15.

Examine how you would feel in Abraham's position. How would

it feel to sit face-to-face with God, the sovereign ruler of the universe and hear bad news? What would you do if God told you the very thing you're praying or the specific promises you are waiting for would not manifest until fifty years from now? Fifty years is only a fraction of four hundred years God presented to Abraham. Moreover, if God told you that the things you are believing Him for won't manifest until you're a hundred years old, or even worse, after your death, would that sit well with you? Would you still have the energy and excitement to pray? Would you still feel love for God and attend fellowship? Would you share your unmanifested dreams with others? Would you be willing to wait? Abraham accepted God's promise without complaint because the patriarch wasn't just only a man of faith but of patience too.

That's exactly what the men and women of faith whose names filled the Holy Bible experienced. Ironically, God's words of delay sat well with them because they had patience, which was their stabilizer through their periods of waiting.

Think about the prophetess Anna (Luke 2:36-38), Simeon (Luke 2: 25–34), and Joseph (Genesis 50: 24–26). Time and space will fail me to list all the people who waited on the Lord to fulfil His promise. The writer of Hebrews also writes of those who never received the promise in their lifetime on earth: "And all these, having obtained a good testimony though faith, did not receive the promise" Hebrews 11:39.

Therefore, I encourage you that as you build your faith, build your patience alongside it, because God's promises don't always manifest overnight. They may delay, seemingly unnecessarily linger, and sometimes even appear to have failed or been unrealistic.

PATIENCE THE STABILIZER

In chapter one, we established that unless faith is firm, confident, steady and stable, it won't be active or functional. Simply stated, it won't work. Also, we discussed the attacks on our faith are used by the enemy to shake, swerve, destabilize or unstable our faith. If any of these negative traits happen, our faith won't be able to function properly. It won't be able to connect to and receive from God. We have to prevent that from happening, and we can't do it by stopping the attacks, because attacks are inevitable. Instead, we prevent our faith from shaking, swerving and destabilizing by adding a stabilizer to it. Patience is that stabilizer like we have established previously.

So what is a stabilizer? Generally speaking, a stabilizer is a piece of equipment that helps make something such as a plane, ship, or electric voltage steady, stable or constant. It also can be like training wheels attached to a child's bicycle to prevent it from falling over. That's exactly the effect patience has on faith. It helps make faith remain steady, stable, confident, unshaken, and unswerving. It prevents it from giving up in the face of strong or troubling oppositions like delays, disappointments and failures.

This is why patience was so important to the patriarchs, Jesus, the apostles, and the early church fathers. Being patient must be important to you too. Now follow me as we dive deeper into why patience as a stabilizer is so important to your faith. Now, let's look into the lives of the two other patriarchs: Isaac and Jacob.

FAILURE BEFORE SUCCESS

Sometimes things fail before they succeed. In fact, you can't conclude things have ultimately failed for you by just one or a couple of attempts you've made. Let's use the life of Isaac to illustrate how success can take time and multiple interventions before fruition.

When Isaac married young Rebekah, it's only normal for the both newlyweds to expect a child immediately after the consummation of their marriage. But that was not the case. Hear what the scripture says about the newlyweds: "Isaac was forty years old when he took Rebekah as wife, the daughter of Bethuel the Syrian of Padan Aram, the sister of Laban the Syrian. Now Isaac pleaded with the LORD for his wife, because she was barren; and the LORD granted his plea, and Rebekah his wife conceived... Isaac was sixty years old when she bore them" (Genesis 25: 20 – 21).

Notice Isaac was forty years old when he married Rebekah. She didn't have any children until he was sixty years old, because she was barren. That is approximately nineteen years of fruitlessness or failed attempts to have children. Relatively, if you're to compare the length of years Isaac and Rebekah had to wait before they could conceive a child to the four hundred years, which we previously discussed, it doesn't sound as extreme. Also, Abraham and Sarah waited twenty-five years from the Lord's promise for Isaac. Nineteen years of waiting may sound pretty reasonable but when you are young, one day of waiting is like a thousand years.

Allow me to put this into perspective. Lily and I got married in the month of August. Our wedding anniversary is August 27th. By September's end that year, we had no sign of pregnancy. The lack of pregnancy didn't really bother either of us since we were enjoying ourselves. Then October passed with no pregnancy. It seemed our attention was somewhat drawn to it like the flash of a bright light in a dark space. However, by mid-November with no pregnancy, it was obvious I was the only one not noticing the delays, disappointments and failed attempts for my wife to conceive over the last two months. One afternoon in November, when Lily realized her monthly period had started again, she broke into tears. My beloved wife became traumatized emotionally for failure to conceive in two months, not two years or twenty years. Well, as I comforted and encouraged her, I found out she had a fear she might have to wait for years like some women do before having children. That thought alone had frightened her, and because she couldn't hide it anymore, she broke into tears. Before I continue, let me state emphatically fear is a trap of the devil! Don't let fear rule in your life. It will limit and torment you to cause you to doubt God's love for you. Eventually, Lily conceived a child, and we rejoiced together like Isaac and Rebekah.

Now let's go back to our Bible narrative. Imagine Rebekah in Lily's condition. Can you comprehend the emotional pain she or any woman in that condition would go through? Rebekah felt forgotten and rejected for nineteen years, not two months. Even more painful was her monthly periods reminding her for nineteen years of how her eggs failed to fertilize every month. Put into months, Rebekah endured her monthly reminder of failure two hundred and twenty-eight times before her success finally came. Wow! Two hundred and twenty-eight failed attempts before the promise came!

That kind of repeated failure would normally break the resolve of any person. Yet, the Bible never records anytime where she or Isaac were troubled or felt broken over their plight. You might say, "Lawrence you don't know that for sure." Well, of course we don't know it for sure, but I believe they didn't falter in faith; otherwise, the Bible would have recorded it. The Bible is not a book that only records the strength of God's people. There are many examples recorded of frustration and questioning faith; the Bible recorded Sarah's impatience, Rachel's jealousy, and Hannah's fretfulness over their childlessness. The Bible also records both the shortcomings and strengths of God's people to prove that all have fallen short and are in need of God's grace and mercy.

However, because both Isaac and Rebekah were patient, they remained hopeful and stable for nineteen years because they knew from Abraham and Sarah's experience, God can make the barren today fruitful tomorrow. You might fail today but succeed tomorrow. The scripture says a righteous man may fall seven times, but he will rise again (see Proverbs 24:16). The patriarch Isaac knew God's faithfulness. He was a living testimony to it. That is why he prayed consistently; the Amplified Bible says Isaac prayed much. "Isaac prayed much to the Lord for his wife because she was unable to bear children; and the Lord granted his prayer, and Rebekah his wife became pregnant" (Genesis 25:21 AMP).

The word "much" can be translated "a lot, often, frequently, a great deal, highly and plenty." In other words, Isaac prayed a lot, often and frequently for his wife. I hope you weren't thinking Isaac prayed only once or a handful of times over nineteen years, and God answered him? Of course, that shouldn't be the attitude of Believer. Isaac was a man of God, which means prayer was a lifestyle for him. Believers today need to be people of constant communication with God too.

The bottom line is, it takes patience to pray often for that length of time, as Isaac did. Many of God's children lose their enthusiasm to pray when they aren't seeing answers quickly. This is simply because they lack patience, the necessary stabilizer of faith. Many believers have given up on praying for something they really knew was God's will for them when they were very close to their miracle manifesting. The result was no manifestation or longer delay. How very sad!

Patience ignores today's failure in order to wait for tomorrow's success. This is why with faith we receive from God, but with faith and patience we receive more. Therefore, develop your patience to the level it can keep you calm and hopeful even when things fail, knowing with God nothing ever fails. It is only a matter of time. With patience and faith, you will be amazed at how things will begin to manifest. I want you to know God is still in control! No failure or delay can stop His promise. That is how patient people think.

Personal Wounds

Sometimes people will hurt or disappoint you. Many even do it intentionally. The pain is magnified when these people are very close to you, and you least expect it from such. When that happens, if you are not a patient person, your response will be very unwise, unpleasant and ungodly. Such negative attitudes or responses may even deprive you of something important to your future. This is one reason we all need patience. It's so important to our faith. Let me illustrate this truth with the life of Jacob. To summarize briefly: Jacob fled Canaan for Haran to escape Esau's conspiracy to kill him after Jacob stole Esau's fatherly blessings. Jacob also left to find a wife from among his maternal uncle's (Laban) house.

Once Jacob arrived at Haran, he met and fell in love with Laban's younger daughter, Rachel. She was in the field where she had come to feed her father's sheep from the well. It was a love at first sight. Jacob loved Rachel and knew for sure she was to be his wife. As soon as word reached Laban that his nephew Jacob was in town, Laban rushed out excitedly to welcome and bring him home. While they were at home, Jacob narrated his plight to Laban. Laban comforted him and made Jacob feel at home. After Jacob had lived with his mother's family for a month, his Uncle Laban offered him a job. Hear that conversation: "Then Laban said to Jacob, 'Because you are my relative, should you therefore serve me for nothing? Tell me, what should your wages be?' Now Laban had two daughters: the name of the elder was Leah, and the name of the younger was Rachel. Leah's eyes were delicate, but Rachel was beautiful of form and appearance. Now Jacob loved Rachel; so he said, 'I will serve you seven years for Rachel, your younger daughter.' And Laban said, 'It is better that I give her to you than I should give her to another man. Stay with me'" (Genesis 29:15-19).

Notice Jacob and Laban had an agreement. Jacob would serve Laban for seven years for the honor of marrying Rachel, his younger daughter. The following passage says: "So Jacob served seven years for Rachel, and they seemed only a few days to him because of the love he had for her" (Genesis 29:20).

Love has the ability to empower us to wait effortlessly. In Jacob's case it not only empowered him to wait, but his love for Rachel made seven years of waiting seem like only a few days. If we can translate this concept to our waiting, we could see our love of God enable us to not only wait, but wait patiently without distress. When we truly love God, waiting for Him becomes nothing to us, like the years were as days to Jacob.

Now comes the big day for Jacob's wedding. Jacob has fulfilled his promised years of labor and has demanded to be wed to his promised wife. In response, Laban threw a feast, a giant wedding party and invited guests. Sadly, something very tragic happened that night. Something that might create a dangerous reaction from most Believers. The bride was brought to Jacob under the cover of darkness and at that moment Laban substituted Leah for Rachel. Laban tricked Jacob and violated their agreement. This was a very gross injustice. By the time Jacob found out of the trickery, it was already morning. It was too late. Jacob was powerless to exchange brides. He was hurt and disappointed knowing this deception was intentional by his own blood relative.

Deception and disappointments like this can happen to anyone. If it was to happen to you, what would you do? Jacob had two options. His first option was to accept his uncle's trickery, keep Leah as his wife, and agree to serve another seven years for his true love, Rachel. His second option was to fight his uncle, reject Leah, and possibly lose Rachel in the end anyway. Either choice was not a good solution. He can hold onto his past anger, or he can chase after a future with Rachel. Scripture says he chose the latter, because Jacob allowed his love for Rachel to influence his emotions, thoughts, and actions in a wise and godly direction. That is exactly how true patience acts as our stabilizer to faith. It influences our emotions, minds and actions to make wise and godly decisions in times of temptations and distress. If Jacob hadn't been patient, he would have lost his true love. This is why patience is so important. We will all meet people like Laban in our Christian walk. If we don't know how to respond to them and press beyond how badly we are hurt or mistreated, we may never reach our positive future goals. Next, let's look at how Jesus and the apostles prized patience in the New Testament.

Fundamental Doctrines

Jesus and the apostles spoke a lot about patience. They also exemplified it in their lifestyles because of its importance. Their thoughts and examples on the theme of patience should help shape our perspective on the importance of patience as Believers. Patience is

a fundamental doctrine in the New Testament. Hear some of the things the New Testament teaches about patience:
- We bear offences or disappointments through patience. Matthew 18:26,29
- We grow Christian fruits or character through patience. Luke 8:15
- We possess or win our soul through patience. Luke 21:19
- We gain experience or character through patience. Roman 5: 4
- We wait for our expectation through patience. Romans 8:25
- Patience is one of the attributes of God. Romans 15:4
- We look for the fruit of patience when identifying or choosing a true minister or church leader. 2 Corinthians 6:4, 12:12, Titus 2:2, 1 Timothy 3:3, 6:11, 2 Timothy 3:10, 2:24
- We wait for and obtain God's promise not only through faith but through patience. Hebrews 6:12, 10:36, James 5:9
- We run the Christian race through patience. Hebrews 12:1
- We mature in faith through patience. James 1:4
- We shall never fall when we add patience to our faith. 2 Peter 1:6, 10
- Jesus takes our patience into account and will reward us for it. Revelation 2:2, 3, 19; 3:10

We should learn to take their words for what it is and see to it that we give patience its proper place in our lives, homes and churches.

Finally, let's look at the place of patience in the early church compared to what we have today.

THE EARLY CHURCH VS TODAY'S CHURCH

Today we live in a culture that seriously undervalues patience as a virtue. This is one of the reasons our world is such a broken place filled with broken people, broken homes, broken churches and broken nations. The current generation doesn't desire to wait for anything. A fast lane generation wants to get to their destiny or destination NOW or NEVER. Sadly, to that generation, patience doesn't sound exciting or appealing and that includes many Christians. In fact, patience is considered by many in the Church today as a weak and powerless virtue. Sadly, many church leaders today share this thought. They take plainly the text "faith is now" to mean if you can't have what you are believing for right now, then you either don't have faith or your faith is too weak. This is a serious misinterpretation of how faith is supposed to work. Regrettably, this belief has stolen the peace and confidence of many Christians, who are now seeking another method to strengthen their faith to receive their manifestation. However, this is not to say that other generations didn't have impatience; every generation has some. It's just that our generation has pushed impatience beyond the limits.

Did you know Church history reveals that the first Christian treatises written on virtue were about patience? Oh yes! The early Believers found patience exciting and praised it publicly, unlike our generation today. Look at how some of the early church fathers praised patience:

- "Patience is the virtue that is peculiarly ours." Origen
- "Patience is the highest virtue." Tertullian
- "Patience is the greatest of all virtues." Lactantius
- "Patience is the way of Christ." Cyprian of Carthage

These godly men and many others were people who faced intense persecutions and martyrdom. In their lifetimes, there were more underground churches than we have today, but the church of Christ grew steadily. Early Christian writers affirmed that in churches that were growing, patience was the important factor.

The bottom line for them and for us is to realize that the best of God is reserved for Believers who will practice their faith with patience (See Isaiah 64:4). I hope our churches and preachers today will emphasize this from the pulpits and their writings like the early church did. Believers need to understand and appreciate the value of waiting. Waiting is not a vain time period; it serves a great and mighty purpose in us according to the first chapter of the Book of James.

CHAPTER 3

Patience

"By your patience possess your souls"
Luke 21:19

In the quoted chapter above from Luke's Gospel, Jesus was asked about the signs that will precede the end of the world and His second coming. Jesus started by enumerating things like the rise of the false Christ, wars and commotions, earthquakes, famines and pestilences, fearful sights and signs from heaven. Then it seems Jesus paused before saying the next words. If He paused, why would He do that? It is because the next words He said applied directly to His disciples, which now includes you and me. His words are very weighty. Let's take a look at what Jesus had to say: "But before all these things, they will lay their hands on you and persecute you, delivering you up to the synagogues and prisons. You will be brought before kings and rulers for my name's sake" (Luke 21:12).

Did you hear that? You will be attacked because of your faith in Christ Jesus. The King James Dictionary defines the word 'persecute' as to "pursue after in order to overtake". In other words, there will be strong oppositional forces pursuing after us to take control of our lives. Let me make it clearer. The goal behind every attack on your life is to discourage you from continuing to trust in God and His Word.

Remember how I said Jesus paused before speaking these words to His disciples because they were very weighty? As Christians this should be our main concern during these end times and nothing else, but does that mean the previous signs He spoke of won't happen to us and as such shouldn't bother us? Let's go back to verse nine for that answer: "But when you hear of wars and commotions, do not be terrified; for these things must come to pass first, but the end will not come immediately" Luke 21:9.

Notice Jesus said when you hear of wars and commotions do not be terrified. In other words, do not panic or be afraid. Don't let these problems bother you. What on earth would make Jesus say we should not be bothered about terrible things like earthquakes, wars, food shortages, diseases, the false Christ and so on? The primary reason rests in the words I highlighted above: when you hear. This means we may only hear of them as news because not all of us will witness wars or some of the other end-time horrors first hand because of the kind of places and times we shall all live in. It has been 2,000 years since Christ rose from the dead, and 2,000 years of living in the end times according to scripture.

Similarly, not every Christian will face physical persecution or injustice for their faith, but be rest assured your faith will face some kind of delay, disappointment or failure as your own price of discipleship. Surely, it will cost you something to follow Jesus. It is even more costly not to follow Him. I say this not to make you afraid because God has not given us the spirit of fear. Fear is a spirit of the devil, and like I said earlier, if you give in to it, it will limit and torment you. Instead, I warn you of the biblical truths behind the cost of discipleship so you are prepared to face them in faith and with patience when the time comes.

Jesus continued His conversation in Luke. His words should comfort, encourage, and give you hope to go through suffering for His name sake: "But it will turn out for you as an occasion for testimony" Luke 21:13.

WOW! Isn't that awesome? Your delays, disappointments or failures are going to turn to a powerful testimony for you and Jesus at the end. That is their purpose, to bring glory to God. I love this awesome promise! It's very comforting for me. It is also why the apostle Paul, who was always in one trouble or another for his faith in Christ, came to a conclusion in Romans where he said, "And we know that all things work together for good to those who love God" (Romans 8:28). No matter what you are going through right now, Jesus and Paul tell you, it's going to be for your good and advantage in the end. You should give God praise for that knowledge.

Is there anything that can give us control over the trials and difficulties Jesus promised would happen to Believers? I mean, what will it take for you and I to survive or outlive these terrible attacks and seemingly unbearable delays, disappointments and failures? Although God is our helper and desires to help us like we discussed earlier, He will never perform our portion of the role set before us. We still have to walk through these trials and attacks. What is our responsibility during the process? Jesus provides the answer: "By your patience possess your souls" Luke 21:19.

The word "possess" here means "to take control, seize, influence, own, hold, win, preserve, keep, obtain, have power over, take over or dominate." The Greek word for "souls" is Psyche and means lives [life]. In fact, other translations of the Bible like NIV, ESV, AMP and NASB rendered it directly as "lives." Examining this verse deeper, we could translate Psyche to also mean "heart," the seat of our emotions, mind and will. In other words, what Jesus is saying is essentially, no matter what attacks come against you, if you are patient, you will take control of your life or heart. Patience enables you to take control over your emotions, thoughts, and actions. When you are able to control these three aspects of life (your response to problems), you will have already overcome most of your circumstances. This is the first step to victory.

Therefore, to take control of your life or heart in times of trial and suffering, you need patience. Consequently, the opposite is also true of impatience. This is why I said in chapter one impatience negatively influences our emotions, minds and actions. Regrettably, when it does, we lose control of our lives and hearts because impatience makes people behave unwisely and ungodly. If we give into impatience, we are in danger of losing the victory and ending in an unhappy life for us.

The Impatient Servant

In Matthew 18, Jesus told the parable of the unforgiving man to illustrate that God has forgiven us so much when compared to what we could ever forgive other people. Although, time and space won't allow for the full scriptural analysis of the ten thousand talents compared to the hundred pence analogy, symbolically the ten thousand talents signified "so much debt he owed" to God. The hundred pence by the other servant signified "so little debt someone owed him". The unforgiving servant is the one who owed his master ten thousand talents (so much debt), but his master pardoned him when he couldn't pay back the debt he owed. Meanwhile his fellow servant owed him hundred pence (little debt), but he refused to forgive him this little debt when his fellow servant was unable to pay it back. In the end of the parable, we learned this unforgiving servant lost everything he had been forgiven because he couldn't forgive the little offense from the people around him. He had been blessed, granted so much forgiveness, but he couldn't forgive others. What an unkind and unforgiving servant!

The question is why did he behave this way? Why did he refuse to forgive his fellow servant? Could it be because the offense was so grave against him? Of course not. Was it because the fellow servant was proud and arrogant to him? Absolutely not!

Give me a moment to help reveal what you may have missed in this parable. To know why this man couldn't pardon his fellow servant of the debt, we must listen to what the hundred pence debtor said when the man confronted him: "So his fellow servant fell down at his feet and begged him saying, have patience with me, and I will pay you all" (Matthew 18:29).

Did you notice the phrase *"have patience with me?"* That would be another way of saying, "give me some time or please wait a little, and I will pay you all." The next verse said he refused. Instead, he threw the debtor into prison until he was able to pay the debt. Simply, the man lost his temper and his refusal meant, "I won't be patient; I want it now." That is the typical response of an impatient person. This Bible parable is often viewed as an unforgiving servant. However, the reason he won't forgive is because he lacks patience. An impatient person always wants it NOW. His impatience didn't only make him lose control of his temperament, mind and actions, but it also ruined his life at the end. Though he got what he wanted urgently from his fellow servant, he lost what he needed from his master. The end result was very tragic.

Interestingly, the same phrase, "have patience with me" is ironically what he asked his master whom he owed ten thousand talents: "The servant therefore fell down before him, saying, 'Master, have patience with me, and I will pay you all'" (Matthew 18:26). Look at his master's response: "Then the master of the servant was moved with compassion, released him, and forgave him the debt" (Matthew 18: 27).

His master responded with compassion. In other words, the master responded in patience as the man requested, and that patience caused him to respond with compassion to forgive the debt. This is the way of Christ, and Believers are expected to walk in His way. Hear what Cyprian of Carthage said: "Patience teaches us to pardon our offenders quickly, and if you yourself should offend, it teaches you to ask pardon, often and with perseverance."

However, one life lesson we can all learn from this bible parable is whenever we act in impatience, we may get what we want NOW, but we will forfeit what we need tomorrow. If we respond with patience in an unfair or difficult situation, we will eventually take control over the current situation and still have victory in the end. This is a double win for our souls.

THE PRODIGAL SON

The prodigal son is one of the most popular stories in the Bible, even non-Christians know it very well. When you think of the prodigal son parable do you ever think of impatience? My guess is probably not. Well, you're not alone. I didn't think of this parable as a story of impatience myself until the Lord drew my attention to it when I was researching this book. The story begins: "And the younger of them said to his father, 'father, give me the portion of goods that falls to me', so he divided to them his livelihood" Luke 15:12.

What the young man was saying here is simply, "father, give me my inheritance." What is an inheritance? An inheritance is any money, property or a title received by a child from its parents after the parents die. Every godly parent owes their children and grandchildren an inheritance because the scripture says, "a good man leaves an inheritance for his children's children" (Proverbs 13:22). This means an inheritance isn't something anyone can earn. Like salvation, it is a gift bestowed on children by their parents. It is to be received as a gift, the same way we receive our salvation as a free gift from God. However, a person can only receive an inheritance once the legal owner dies, or if he decides to give it out in their lifetime willfully. As you can see in this young man's case, he stepped ahead and demanded it. Let me put another way, he wanted his future portion NOW. This was not a practice among the ancient Jewish people, neither do I know of any culture globally where this is a practice regarding inheritance.

Apparently, his behavior of asking for something that will be rightly given him later after his father is dead defines one word – *impatience*. He cannot wait. The father never made any attempt to stop him, because you cannot stop any impatient man from doing or saying something they want.

So, the prodigal son got what he wanted and off he went into a foreign nation where he began a wasteful life. Are you surprised he did what he did with his life treasure? Do you think if you demanded your inheritance now like he did that you would use it wisely? Well, I'm afraid your actions won't be any different from his, because an impatient person does not have control over their actions. An impatient person is like a drunkard; he has no control or power over his actions. Drunks are only in their right senses once the effect of the alcohol has cleared, and usually when it wears off, they regret their actions. An impatient man isn't any different. Hear what King Solomon penned thousands of years ago concerning this young man and anyone who will behave like him: "An inheritance gained hastily at the beginning will not be blessed at the end" (Proverbs 20:21).

Did you catch that? When you get an inheritance sooner than you are supposed to, out of impatient desperation, the end is always disastrous. No one wants that. Impatience made the prodigal son lose everything he gained from his father to a wasteful lifestyle in a foreign nation. However, when it dawned on him that everything was gone, he began to properly reason again and made a decision to return home.

Although, the father welcomed him back with such great compassion and even threw a big party for him which made his elder brother angry and jealous, in the end, the young man had no further inheritance from his father. Hear how the father comforted the elder brother with this word: "But as soon as this son of yours came, who has devoured your livelihood with harlots, you killed the fatted calf for him. And he said to him, 'Son, you are always with me, and all that I have is yours'" Luke 15:30–31.

Did you hear that? All that the father had left now belonged to his first son. The prodigal son had a tough lesson. Because he got what he thought he wanted, he forfeited what he would need in the future. Additionally, because he took his portion early, it didn't have time to multiply, and he actually received less of an inheritance than he would have if he had waited. What a poor choice! Remember when Israel pressed God to give them a king before His time? It ended in disaster for them as a nation. Impatience is a trap and a very dangerous one. Beware!

THE STRONG WILL FAINT

Do you know that you need more than determination, courage and strong will power to succeed in God's kingdom? Oh yes. Don't get me wrong; these are good attributes to help people succeed in every endeavor. However, they are not enough because at some point, we shall all face the unbearable. Perhaps it's something or someone we can't put up with, or an unexpected catastrophe. If you haven't already experienced it, you will face it someday soon. When that day comes, you will know even the strong can faint.

I don't want you to be tempted to think the reason you failed or gave up on things you really knew were God's will for you was because you are not a strong person, as defined by having determination, courage and strong-willed power. The truth is at some point, every Believer feels tired, exhausted, wearied, weakened, defeated, overcome and discouraged, especially when we face unbearable attacks. When the attacks are long in duration, lasting years or decades, the resolve of a Believer is often worn down. Sadly, some Believers read scriptures like Proverbs 24:10, "If you faint in the day of adversity, your strength is small," and feel they are not measuring up or are weak compared to others. Often, those we admire for their strength today have fought the battle of giving up. Many are still fighting the battle in arenas we don't see. Thankfully, we have a great, high priest, Jesus Christ, who overcame in every way as we have been tempted, and through Him, He helps us overcome the unbearable.

Without Jesus and His help from above, even the most devout would give up when they face agonizing situations. The reason is because everybody has a breaking point. It is a point where people give up their grit or determination, courage, and will power when they experience the unbearable. The definition of "unbearable" often varies person to person, and what is unbearable for one may be easier for another. Never judge another person's trial or their ability to carry it. Remember Aaron, Hur, and the seventy elders we discussed in chapter one? Courage, determination and will power weren't enough. Look at other strong people in the Bible who encountered the unbearable at some point in their life:
- King Saul feared his people would abandon him in the face of their enemy and compromised (see 1 Samuel 13).
- Naomi felt the Lord was against her and set to return to her nation (see Ruth 1).
- King David the great warrior ran away from his once little boy Absalom (see 2 Samuel 15 and 16).
- Abraham and Sarah temporarily broke out of God's will for their life (see Genesis 16)

- Peter denied the Lord thrice (see Matthew 26).

The list of names who were strong heroes of Israel or faith who experienced failure is long. Let's look again at Proverbs 24:10, "If you faint in the day of adversity, your strength is small." Did you know this verse has a complementary scripture in Proverb 24:16? "For the righteous man may fall seven times and rise again."

Isn't that encouraging? The righteous man fell, then he rose again – several times. It should give you hope. It's okay to fall and doesn't take away from your righteousness to fall. Everyone will fall or give up at some point in his/her life without divine strength and deliverance. Thankfully, we serve a great God who never faints or gives up: "Have you Know? Have you not heard? The everlasting God, the LORD, The Creator of the ends of the earth, neither faints nor is weary. His understanding is unsearchable" Isaiah 40:28.

Everyone else will faint: become tired, exhausted, wearied and give up except that God supplied them strength. The Bible says youth symbolizes strength: "The Glory of young men is their strength" (Proverb 20:29). In other words, strong people are youthful people irrespective of their age. Think about Caleb. At 80 years old, he was as strong as 40 and took his inheritance in the Promised Land with the vigor and energy of a youth. However, if people rely on their flesh or self, if they depend on their own abilities of determination, courage or will power, they shall grow faint. They will get discouraged, break down, and give up in the race. Isaiah said about the strong or youthful people: "Even the youths shall faint and be weary, and the young men shall utterly fall" (Isaiah 40:30).

But now see the passages before and after that verse 30: "He [God] gives power to the weak, and to those who have no might. He increases strength" (Isaiah 40:29). Did you catch that? God gives power to the weak. God increases and renews their strength so that they can fly like eagles again and overcome every storm. With God's strength, they never back down when they face insurmountable obstacles. If you are currently feeling defeated, discouraged, and want to give up, these words should cheer and encourage you.

Sometimes, Lily and I often wonder where on the earth are we finding the courage to continue what we are doing for the Lord when we face seemingly unbearable and insurmountable obstacles. Of course, we just know the Lord is always fueling and servicing us for His work as He has promised to do. But the truth is God doesn't just fuel anybody.

Otherwise, people, including His children, won't be giving up too often. Who are those that will receive divine strength and deliverance from the unbearable? Who God will refuel and sustain? Here is the answer: "But those who *wait* on the Lord shall renew their strength; they shall mount up with wings like eagles. They shall run and not be weary. They shall walk and not faint" (Isaiah 40:29, 31 italics added). "Because you have kept my Word of *passionate patience*, I'll keep you safe in the time of testing" (Revelation 3:10 MSG). While the passage from Revelation refers to the great tribulation that characterizes the end of the world; however, it is also how God works to save His people from any trial too great for them, see 1 Corinthians 10:13.

From the scriptures above, you will notice God's people who will walk in *patience* will be the ones God gives extra strength to face their unbearable and deliver them from it when necessary. To *wait* on the Lord means, "to expect, look and trust patiently on the Lord." In other words, it means *patience*. If we patiently trust in the Lord during seasons of great trials and suffering, Believers can take control of their lives and circumstances and prevent a breaking point from occurring.

Who Appoints the Time?

One of the questions Jesus disciples asked Him on a couple of occasions was a matter of timing. They were eager to know when would Jesus return again, when would the world end and when would He restore His kingdom. Jesus' answer to these questions all through scripture makes it clear who is in control of times and season. Father God is the one who sets and controls the timing of events in the world and in our lives. Paul the apostle also affirmed this truth strongly in his epistles to the Thessalonians Church (see 1 Thessalonians 5:1). Hear Jesus' exact response to these questions: "But of the day and hour no one knows, not even the angels of heaven, but by my Father only" (Matthew 24: 36). And He said to them, "It is not for you to know times or seasons which the Father has put in His own authority" (Acts 1: 7). In a different sense, this is similar to the questions most Believers ask today. When will my delay, disappointment or failure end?

A parent in our school approached me one morning. She wanted me to keep her in prayers, especially for a business delay her husband was facing. When she noticed my friendly response to her request, she started sharing how the delay is affecting their entire family finances.

At this time, I discerned she also needed some encouragement, which I gave her. I ended my words with the popular phrase, "this too shall pass" and things will be great again!

"When?" She asked.

My reply was, "Leave the when for God and focus on the moment, for God makes things beautiful in their time (Ecclesiastes 3:11)." This is the message for you too, leave the when for God and focus on today. If you are focused on the when, you won't be able to take control of things today. Essentially, if you are asking God when the promise will come or when your prayer will be answered, you are attempting to set the time according to your will. Believers shouldn't focus on the *"when"* but should focus on the fact God's timing is always perfect. When we remember God's timing is perfect, the "when question" will not matter, because our confidence rests in the fact: it will be done. Think about the story of the prodigal son. When he demanded his own time for his inheritance, his end was bad. If he had patience to wait to receive his inheritance at the appointed time in the future, he would not have squandered his wealth.

I want you to underline or write out these words if you can, **"God never delays. He never disappoints. God never fails!"**

Meditate on these truths. They will change your life!

THE DEATH OF LAZARUS

When talking about God's perfect timing, we can deepen our understanding of His timing from how Christ responded to the news of Lazarus sickness. Do you remember the story? Lazarus and his two sisters, Mary and Martha, were very dear friends of Jesus. It happened one day Lazarus became sick. His sisters sent a message to the Lord stating, "Lord, he whom you love is sick." When Jesus received the message, He shared it with His disciples. Yet, Jesus deliberately stayed away two more days before going to Bethany, the town where Lazarus and his sisters lived.

Let me just quickly counter one lie of the devil before continuing. Sometimes, the enemy wants you to think that God doesn't love you because of the delay you are facing. That is a capital LIE. The next time he comes pushing this thought into your heart, don't give him any attention, because you are so loved by God unconditionally. God desires the best for you always. How do I know that? One reason is because

God loved Lazarus and his sisters, yet He didn't respond to their plea immediately. The Scriptures says: "Now Jesus loved Martha and her sister and Lazarus. So, when He heard that he was sick, He stayed two more days in the place where He was" (John 11:5-6). Did you catch that? He loved them and that's why Jesus delayed coming. Their brother was going to die, yet Jesus didn't budge. He knew Lazarus' death would glorify God. But when examining the scriptures on how his death would glorify God, we see something interesting in these verses. It says "Jesus loved Martha." Mary often sat at the feet of the master while he taught. She was the woman who anointed Jesus before his death. Mary was sensitive to the Spirit of God and knew of his love for her. But Martha had focused on her works. She complained against Mary resting at the feet of the savior while she worked. Martha was busy serving the Lord and didn't know Lord's heart was to serve her. Martha didn't understand the personal love of God for her. Lazarus' death was about to change her understanding of God's power and love for her.

Now let me ask you, as a Christian, what do you desire in your life to change or be resurrected from the dead for God's glorify? The pain and struggle you are enduring now is not because God doesn't love you. You are enduring the experience BECAUSE He loves you. He wants to use your negative experiences to show you His love, faithfulness, patience and put a new song in your mouth. A song that will make you and those who hear it glorify God. I think you should pause right now, close this book for a minute, and praise the Lord for the depths of His great love for you.

Jesus and His disciples arrived exactly two days after He got the news of His friend's sickness. By this time Lazarus was already dead. He'd been buried four days ago. The Bible records Lazarus stunk already, as his body was decaying. Upon Jesus' arrival, Martha and Mary came differently to welcome Him, but they both said essentially the same thing to Him: "Lord, if you had been here, my brother would not have died" (John 11:21, 32).

Their statement implied Jesus had intentionally delayed, which he did. However, there was also the accusation was He came late. If only Jesus had come sooner, their brother would not have died. To put it another way, "Lord it is your fault our brother died because you weren't here for him. You didn't love him enough to come quickly."

Maybe you can relate with the sisters' accusation? Have there being times in your life when you felt it was God's fault you lost something or someone dear because He didn't show up, or maybe He was late in responding to your cry for help? Do you feel at times, if God doesn't show up now, things will go out of control? Well then, be of good cheer. It's not over. It's not out of control. Jesus is never late. The King of kings is in control of the universe. Things will never be out of His control. Trust Him and relax. See what He did for Lazarus to understand God is never late.

The end of Lazarus' story concludes with Jesus calling him back to life from the grave. Jesus demonstrated to Martha and Mary He was in full control, even over death. He verified His love for Lazarus and them through His miracle. Jesus also showed them He has the perfect time for doing things. That time may not feel right, or it may seem too late, but Jesus knows the timing more perfectly than Martha, Mary or even you and I.

If a man who was dead, buried, and decaying was resurrected back to life after four days of being in a grave, then there is nothing that has died, been lost or decaying in your life that Jesus cannot restore to life. This includes your marriage, children, health, finances, business or ministry. Jesus is the **Resurrection** and the **Life**. That means nothing dies in Him. Nothing placed in His hands can be lost, and no one in His kingdom will ever truly die.

If life hasn't gone according to your planned timetable, don't be bitter about it. Patiently wait on the Lord. He will provide and make a way in His time. We cannot manipulate or push God to change His mind. There is no work or effort you can do to merit His favor to change your situation to your timeline. All you can do is wait patiently for His time knowing, it will always be beautiful at the end and for your ultimate good. God loves you.

GOD WAITS FOR US

God doesn't just call us to be patient while He is excluded from it. No. Patience is a core aspect of God. In short, the Bible calls Him, "a God of patience" (Romans 15:4). When God waits for us, He does it with intentionality, passion, and love for us. His patient nature is characterized in how He deals with us every day and even in the establishment of His kingdom here on earth. God is not in a hurry over anything. No doubt, without patience the Lord could not maintain His unchanging love, sovereign control and faithfulness towards His people. The reason is simple: we are a rebellious people in nature. We are soon to fall short of His standards. Think about the Israelites' relationship with God for a moment!

David declared in Psalm 103:10, "He [God] has not dealt with us according to our sins, nor punished us according to our iniquities." Again, the Psalmist declared: "if You, Lord, should mark iniquities, O Lord, who could stand?" (Psalm 130:3).

If we who are God's people are sincere, Believers should know that we cannot stand boldly in God's presence apart from what Jesus Christ has done for us through His death and resurrection. Even with this gift, many are still finding it hard to believe and receive boldness to come into God's presence to seek help in times of trouble, because the devil has blinded their minds about how patient and loving God is towards them. God is waiting for people to come and receive the gift of forgiveness He provided through His Son, Jesus Christ.

However, God desires to produce His grace of patience in us so that Believers can grow into mature and completely anointed children. This is one reason God the Holy Spirit is dwelling inside Believers. He is like a seed of patience planted within our spirit to produce the fruit of patience manifesting outward in our minds, emotions, and actions. The more we allow patience to grow and manifest in our lives, the more Christ-like we become. This is why God is inviting Believers daily to drink from His fountain of patience to empower us to live like Jesus did. Patience will enable us to treat others and our circumstances with grace and love.

CHAPTER 4

DECEPTIVE PATIENCE

"Therefore by their fruits you will know them."
Matthew 7: 20

Patience involves more than mere waiting for what you want to arrive. When you understand all the aspects of patience, which include endurance, long suffering, forbearance, steadfastness and perseverance, then you will know patience is about the attitudes, behaviors and actions when one encounters situations, things or people we do not like in our waiting seasons. Don't forget patience influences our souls: emotions, mind and will. Biblical patience isn't being passive in waiting seasons, instead it's being active. Patience sets us on the run, getting ready for the promise, chasing after, and ultimately conforms us into the image of Christ. Hear what God told the prophet Habakkuk: "Then the Lord answered me and said: 'Write the vision and make it plain on tablets, that he may run who reads it. For the vision is yet for an appointed time; But at the end it will speak, and it will not lie. Though it tarries, wait for it; because it will surely come, it will not tarry'" (Habakkuk 2:2-3).

Notice the Lord said, **"though it tarries,"** which means it will be delayed. God reminds him to wait for it, because it will surely come. Whether God's promise will come is no longer the focus of the question. The main question is, "why the delay?" The delay or waiting season is the testing season, where you find out more about yourself. Are you a fake or authentic Christian? Are you just in this for the personal advantage, or you truly love the Lord? The Lord already knows who you are and what you will be in the end, but we lack the understanding of our true motives, selfishness, or pride that still need to be corrected in our lives so that we may draw closer to the person and image of Jesus. In your season of delay, your behavior will identify your heart. It is not only the length of the delay that will try you, but the type of delay you shall face will also affect you. Therefore, how you behave in your waiting season matters, because it doesn't just tell whether you are a patient person or not. It demonstrates the type of Christian you truly are, and even if you are not a Christian. Remember: ***By their fruits you will know them.***

This is why anything short of a godly behavior while waiting is deceptive and is a false practice of patience. Ungodly behavior will never lead to the promise. Instead, it will lead you to ruin. Deception brings destruction, which is why times of delay are so valuable. Times of intense pressure and delay uproot any self-deception we were trying to hide or ignore while wearing our Christian-mask. But God loves Truth and authenticity. He loves us too much to let us live a lie or hide a lie in our heart. He will place us in uncomfortable situations to reveal any deception to us in order to help us grow and trust Him more.

People traveling a path of deception either in ignorance or deliberately end up in pain, frustration, and misery. Most are blindsided when they are suffering from deception. Pause and reflect on the bible parable about the five foolish virgins. They didn't use their waiting season wisely to prepare for the bridegroom.

Let me illustrate this further with the exhortation that the apostle James gave to early Christians who were facing suffering while waiting for Jesus' second coming. "Therefore be patient, brethren, until the coming of the Lord. See how the farmer waits for the precious fruit of the earth, waiting patiently for it until it receives the early and latter rain" James 5:7.

Notice after James calls them to be patient like a farmer. Next James said, *"see how the farmer waits."* How do farmers wait patiently for their harvest? If you're familiar with farming or have elementary knowledge of it practices, you know how they wait. However, I want you to know that the *"patient waiting"* of the farmer is not passive but active. There is a lot a farmer does during this season of waiting before the harvest. Farmers waters the crops, pull up weeds, stake growing stems, control pests, and the list goes on. These are different activities farmers engage as part of the process to allow proper germination and development of their plants. Farmers are active while patiently waiting for the harvest.

Similarly, before we can have our harvest, there are attitudes and behaviors God desires us to express as part of our character growth: gratitude, joyfulness, soberness, faithfulness, humility, obedience and more. Also, there are also behaviors God wants us to get rid of similar to the pest control the farmers perform to remove unwanted invasion or destruction of their harvest: impatience, greed, pride, selfishness, jealousy, anger and more. If these unhealthy mindsets and behaviors grow within us, they have the potential to destroy our harvest.

Now let's discuss some of the negative attitudes or pests some Christians display in their season of waiting which have the potential to deny them of their promised harvest.

WAITING AND COMPLAINING

Complaining is one of the most infectious negative attitudes. It spreads like the most notorious weed in a garden. The word complaining can also be rendered as grumbling or murmuring. It might also mean to be unhappy or unsatisfied by something or someone.

Regrettably, if believers don't develop patience to control their hearts, they will begin to feel unhappy or unsatisfied with God. The resulting emotion causes many to complain about the things God isn't doing in their lives. When God does something but it's not happening at their pace, they complain and grumble against His timing. When God appears to not be moving at all, their complaints and murmurs against God become very loud. Scriptures tell us God condemns complaining. The reason is because when we complain or grumble, it means we have quickly forgotten God's past goodness and faithfulness in our lives. In other words, we are saying God doesn't care or He is not in control of things as He claims. This lie is a great contempt to God. (See Exodus 15:24, 16:2, Number 14:1–3, 37). "And do not grumble, as some of them did – and were killed by the destroying angel" (1 Corinthians 10:10 CEV). Israelites who grumbled or complained in the wilderness were killed by a destroying angel sent by God. Sadly, the complainers never entered the Promised Land. They never reaped their harvest, and their end was tragic.

Several times the Israelites complained and murmured against God despite all that God had done for them. They quickly forgot the miracles of provision God had given them: the ten plagues, the parting of the Red Sea, fresh water, and even food. When any slight delay or obstacle appeared, instead of believing the God who had delivered them from the strongest army in the world would provide for them again, they quickly turned to complaining about their current situation or lack. Their focus on their flesh and feelings rebelled against the love and provision God had provided over and over again. Whenever they were in need, they forget the previous miracle God did.

Sadly, Israel's old pattern is pretty much the attitude of most believers today. They can't remember anything except the moment of NOW. This kind of forgetful attitude and ingratitude bears grave consequences before God and is why the apostle Paul warned the Corinthian Church with the above verse from 1 Corinthians 10:10. God is able to help us overcome. However, the Old Testament is a reminder for us today: those who are faithful and patient enter the Promised Land; those who are faithless and complaining reap destruction.

Also the apostle James also warned early Believers who were facing trial and suffering to stop complaining among themselves: "Do not complain, brethren, against one another, so that you (yourselves) may not be judged. Look! The Judge is (already) standing at the very door" (James 5:9 AMP).

This warning applies directly to Believers today. We are warned to refrain completely from the attitude of complaining whenever we are waiting on God to act in our circumstances. Instead of complaining, Believers should begin to thank God for the past things He has done. Reminding ourselves of the past miracles, fulfilled promises, and work of God in our lives help us remember God's faithfulness and remain patient while we wait for our current promise to be fulfilled. This is my own antidote for complaining, and I highly recommend it.

WAITING BUT NOT READY

The time of waiting is not a time to sit idle, cross fingers, and do nothing. It's a time to get ready for the promise. Nobody is ready at the moment when a promise is given. In fact, that's why it's a promise: it's futuristic and you have to get yourself ready to receive it. So whenever God says He "will" do something for you, find out what you should be "doing" to equip yourself for that promise.

In Genesis 37:5–9, God showed Joseph his future twice through dreams. Essentially, God gave Joseph a promise through his dreams. However, Joseph prepared for God's promise in a hard way, facing disappointments from his own blood brothers, trafficked on a foot with chains to Egypt where he served as a bondman manager in Potiphar's house. Later he was tested for moral purity through his master's wife and landed in jail for refusing to compromise his belief in God's righteous standards. Finally, in jail Joseph helped a guy who happened to be Pharaoh's chief butler. Joseph asked the butler to use his influence with Pharaoh to help him out of prison, but for two years the guy forgot Joseph completely. Then suddenly, God had the butler remember him, thrusting him into his promised destiny.

The truth is everything Joseph went through before God's promise manifested was terrible. It took great grace to bear up through the trials without misbehaving. However, every trial prepared Joseph for leadership. God knew Joseph wasn't prepared to lead Egypt before the trials he endured when He showed Joseph his destiny. Between the promise and the manifestation, Joseph had a choice to either endure God's refining process to prepare him for his destiny or give up and forfeit his harvest.

This concept is the same the way God prepares Believers for His promises today. Jesus said the qualification to lead begins with first being willing to serve (See Matthew 20:25 – 28). The time of "serving" is the time you encounter things that you won't be able to tolerate, but to please God we have to endure them patiently and respond in love. Our response of love isn't for the painful situation or the difficult people. Our response in love is rooted in our love for God and not out of obligation. If through patience we serve God with gratitude, thanksgiving and praise, God will use periods of delay, disappointment, or failure to build a strong inner character with the necessary skills to handle the next season, just like He did for Joseph.

For instance, between when God revealed His plan of ministry to me and when I eventually started my work was a span of eight years. Why did it take that long? Was it because I was rebelling against God's purpose for my life? Not at all! In fact, I was too desperate and passionate to begin what God had called me to do (to minister Christ and add value to people in Africa and the world). So what stalled me for those eight years? It was simply that I was not ready. The Lord used those eight years to grow and mature my faith and leadership skills through many opportunities. I became planted in a local church, served in various department of the church like cleaning toilets, cutting grasses, cleaning the sanctuary, visiting new converts and first timers, evangelizing in the street, serving in prayer bands, leading house fellowships, teaching at and leading children's ministry, preparing Sunday school curriculum, attending several youth camps, conferences and local Bible School run by my church then. The list goes on.

Conversely, I could have sat idle doing nothing but waiting passively for God's promises to somehow come to pass in my life. If that had been my attitude, I would still be waiting with nothing to show. If I had tried to force my destiny and jump straight into the position I was called, I would have been ill prepared to enter into it. The result would've been my shame and disgrace, not being fully equipped for the position. Think about the Israelites. Preparation precedes glorification. Wherever you find lack of preparation, disappointments, shame and disgrace is always the result. Sadly, many are waiting, but few are ready.

This is why if you are a single waiting to get married, I strongly recommend you use your waiting season to prepare yourself to be a good wife or husband. Learn godly communication and parenting skills because the future Mr. or Mrs. Right will surely come, as well as your kids. The real question is will you be prepared to handle this level of a committed relationship when it comes? Are you cultivating the skills necessary to create a thriving partnership with another person? Good communication, financial wisdom, mutual respect, expressing gratitude and thankfulness, self-sacrifice, trust, and loyalty are just a few of the talents necessary for a successful relationship. When you have a promise from God like receiving a marital partner, take it with confidence. Since your promise is coming, are you prepared?

THE FOOLISH VIRGINS

The five foolish virgins are a typical biblical example of people who failed to get ready in their waiting season. In Matthew 25, Jesus gave a parable where He compares the kingdom of heaven to be ten virgins who took their lamps to meet the bridegroom. While this parable explicitly teaches valuable lessons on the importance of the spiritual readiness, it could also teach an important lesson about getting ready for any opportunity that presents itself. It was Abraham Lincoln, the sixteenth president of the United States of America who said, "I will study and wait until the opportunity comes." The importance of getting ready for the promise during the season of waiting cannot be overemphasized.

In the virgin parable there are ten virgins eligible to marry the bridegroom, but they had to wait for him. As was the practice in the ancient Jewish culture, the groom often arrived late at night. Jacob's marriage to Leah reflects this concept. While this was the practice of the groom to come at night, in this parable, we were told the bridegroom *"tarried,"* which meant he delayed and was later than expected. Automatically, the brides had to wait longer than originally expected, and in the process, they all fell asleep. What happened next distinguished the virgins into wise and foolish.

At midnight the bridegroom finally arrived and a call was made to alert the virgins. Immediately, all ten awoke and turned up their lamps. Five noticed immediately their lamps were going out because they ran out of oil to burn. Sadly, they didn't have any extra oil to refuel the lamps because they forgot to bring extra oil. But even worse, these virgins didn't use the bridegroom's delay as an opportunity to prepare by trying to go out and buy more oil. Instead, we are told they slept when the bridegroom delayed. This made them foolish.

However, five virgins brought extra oil. In other words, they were prepared for the delay. When the bridegroom arrived, the virgins with the extra oil, refueled their lamps and went out to meet him. At that moment, the foolish virgins pleaded with the wise to give them some oil, but they refused because the oil wouldn't be enough if it was shared. Instead, the five wise virgins advised them to go back to town and buy oil. Straightway, the foolish virgins left. The foolish virgins did the right thing in going to buy the oil, but they did it at the wrong time. Many of us are guilty of similar problems, we do the right things but not at the right time: "And while they went to buy, the bridegroom came and they that were READY went in with him to the marriage and the door was shut" (Matthew 25: 10).

Did you notice the word **READY**? The scripture emphasizes the word "ready" because the people who receive the promises of God are those who are prepared. What distinguished the five wise virgins from the foolish ones? They were ready and prepared for their bridegroom, having secured extra oil for the long delay before he came.

Are you ready for what you're waiting for? Before you rush to say yes, look at a deeper meaning of the word ready. Ready means finished and available for use. When reflecting on whether or not we are ready, we need to ask ourselves, "have we finished developing our skills and available for God to use in ministry, marriage, business, leadership position or for greater influence in what God has called us to do?

Unfortunately, God isn't going to wait forever. There is a deadline. Even God's grace has a deadline. Think about the people who missed opportunities in life simply because they were not ready when it came. The season of waiting is to ensure everything we need to do on our part is completed, not left undone.

WAITING IN HOPELESSNESS

Hope is a confident expectation that God's promise will be received, and it's an inherent characteristic of patience. The Bible says: "But if we hope for what is still unseen by us, we wait for it with patience and composure" (Romans 8:25 AMP). In other words, hope is one of the reasons we want to wait patiently for the manifestations of God's promise, even if it is going to take forever to happen. We know our hope in Christ and His promises won't disappoint nor will it put us to shame. However, in our waiting season, hope through the power of the Holy Spirit will keep our hearts in peace and joy. That means hope casts away worry, anxiety and fear. Hope casts away doubt.

Conversely, if we are not confident God will perform what He promises in His word, we become troubled, discouraged, and give up. A hopeless person cannot wait on God. Even if he feigns it outwardly, it will not profit any good in the end, because being hopeless is being doubtful. Whenever doubt sets in, we have disconnected ourselves from receiving from God by faith.

Don't lose hope, because the promise is yet to manifest. Remember Abraham? The scripture said of him who was in a hopeless situation that he remained hopeful that what God had promised, He also was able to bring it to pass. Abraham never considered the infertility of Sarah's womb, because he knew God was faithful. Abraham also knew it is impossible for God to lie. I encourage you to remain hopeful.

The bottom line is, if you are really waiting for God, you will be hopeful because hope and patience are inseparable. I love this quote from Tertullian about patience: *"Hope is patience with the Lamp lit."* Keep your hope alive. Your miracle is closer now than it was yesterday.

WAITING IN FEAR

Fear is a weapon of the enemy to control our lives. It makes us doubt God's goodness and faithfulness. Fear grows in us when we listen to the devil or faithless people. The enemy wants to control the outcome of your life by putting fear in your heart. If he succeeds, he will direct your thoughts and actions as he wills. You will become like a puppet on a string, being manipulated and controlled by your fears. The end result will be misery, pain and regrets. This is because fear limits us from going forward in faith and courage to do what God has called us to do or be who He has called us to be. Many believers are where they are today, because they fear the unknown. They are focusing only on their abilities, resources and inadequacies alone. Similar to the ten spies who brought an evil report to Moses, when we focus on only our strengths and weaknesses, we do not see God's promises or miracles. Fear blinds us from remembering there is more to the equation for success than our input alone. If I had followed fear, I wouldn't be in ministry today or be where I'm presently in most areas of my life. Fear steals our peace and paralyzes us.

How do we overcome fear in our season of waiting? We must face it head on in faith and courage. Be encouraged by David's declaration of faith in a time of strong intimidation from his enemy: "The LORD is my light and my salvation; whom shall I fear? The LORD is the strength of my life; of whom shall I be afraid?" (Psalm 27:1).

Even as David declared his faith in God's power, he still needed courage to wait for God's manifestation as he faced his enemies. Read his latter words: "Wait on the Lord; be of good courage, And He shall strengthen your heart; Wait, I say, on the Lord!" Psalm 27:14.

It takes courage to wait for the manifestation of God's power in our lives, even when we have made declarations of faith like David. Courage is not the absence of fear. It is the determination to face what is intimidating even when we feel fear in the process. Think about God's instruction to Moses when they were pinned in by the Red Sea on one side with Pharaoh's army advancing toward them. "Go forward," God commanded in the face of fear.

Fear is an emotion all people feel at some time. The big question is whether or not we allow fear to control our actions? Can we move forward and do what God commanded in faith and courage like Moses did? Do we remind ourselves in times of opposition and intense struggle to be of good cheer and have courage like David?

Let's examine another biblical king. King Saul was waiting for Samuel in Gilgal. Samuel instructed him to wait for him for seven days until Samuel came (see 1 Samuel 13:8). On the seventh day, when King Saul didn't see Samuel, he allowed himself to be controlled by fear of the Philistines. The Philistine armies were like the sand on the sea shore, intimidating Saul and his followers. Being impatient, King Saul did wait for Samuel, even though he did wait seven days. When Samuel was delayed, Saul began to justify performing Samuel's job for him. Then he did the unthinkable, King Saul thought to circumvent the priesthood and offer burnt sacrifices and peace offerings to God, which was only lawful for priests. Ironically, as soon as Saul completed his sacrifices, Samuel arrived. This means Samuel's delay was mere hours not days in coming. Saul's impatience caused him to sin against God and was great enough for God to take his kingdom away. If he'd only patiently waited just a few more hours instead of allowing fear to manipulate him.

One lesson to learn from this story in 1 Samuel 13:1-14 is in your waiting season, never allow fear to control you. Fear will either cause you to move in the wrong direction or it will paralyze you completely. Fear will steal your peace today and your future tomorrow. King Saul is a perfect example of fear causing failure. Listen to the outcome of God's verdict on Saul's fear and lack of waiting on the Lord: "And Samuel said unto Saul 'You have done foolishly. You have not kept the commandment of the Lord your God, which He commanded you, But now your kingdom shall not continue. The Lord has sought for Himself a man after His own heart, and the Lord has commanded him to be commander over His people, because you have not kept what the Lord commanded you'" (1Samuel13:13-14).

What a high price Saul paid because of fear. He lost a future blessing of royalty for himself and his family. One implication from this story is because of Saul's impatient actions, none of his children, including the righteous Jonathan, would ever be heir to the throne or become king of Israel. Saul lost his reign forever.

When we allow fear to control us during our season of patient waiting, we will end up compromising God's standards. We will also violate His directions and instructions like Saul did. The penalty for allowing fear to control you is high, and in the end is also always worse than if you had simply patiently waited for God in spite of the fear.

WAITING WITHOUT JOY

Joy is an inner peace and delight we receive as a result of our salvation in Christ and being in fellowship with God. Joy is a sign of being in fellowship with the Lord (see John 15:1–11). This means as long as we abide in our fellowship with God through our waiting season, nothing can ruin our joy. Not even the unbearable can concur with your joy in Jesus.

This doesn't mean once in a while we won't experience sorrow or grieve in our heart. But that temporary sorrow or grief will not remain. The joy of the Lord will be our strength. If for some reason, you stay in a position of sorrow and feel no joy, you may need to examine your fellowship with God. Whenever a Believer lacks joy, it's usually an indication of broken fellowship with the Lord. Joy is a necessity when patiently waiting. Why? It's because the joy of the Lord is our strength. Joy helps Believers to move on cheerfully, without complaint, even in the face of unbearable circumstances.

When Nehemiah led his building team to build the broken walls of Jerusalem, they faced a lot of attacks. Some evil people threaten their lives, but Nehemiah and his faithful workers continued the work. To the glory of God, they completed the wall in the face of their enemies. Where did they find strength to win such victory? Their secret is in Nehemiah 8:10: "...Do not sorrow, for the joy of the Lord is your strength."

Don't wait to be joyful after your miracle comes. Stay joyful while you wait for your miracle. In doing so, you are not only abiding in fellowship with the Lord, but you are gaining more strength to face your circumstances. A joyful Christian is a powerful Christian.

WAITING WITHOUT PRAYER

It was Leonard Ravenhill, the great English revivalist of the 20th century who said, "If you're not praying you're playing". This is so true! Let me state here bluntly that, *waiting without praying is wasting time without knowing.* God knows all our needs, yet He still commanded us to pray. But, why is prayer important to God? Since He already knows our needs, why can't He simply just meet them for us? This is the question many people ask, including Christians. Prayer seems like a burden. God created us for relationship and saved us through Jesus Christ for relationship. Our relationship with God is so important to Him, and that's exactly what prayer helps to develop for us. Prayer helps to develop our understanding of our relationship with God. So whether you are praying for your personal needs or for God's kingdom in general, you are developing and maintaining your relationship with God. Prayer is very important in our waiting seasons.

However, our prayers also go beyond just building relationship. They invite God into our situations. The fact that you are waiting isn't enough reason for God to act on your behalf. Just as fasting alone doesn't cause God to respond to your request, time spent waiting or fasting also requires prayer. Prayer initiates a response from God as part of our relationship with Him. God knows what we need, but most times He wants to be invited into our situation through prayer before He intervenes. Prayer demonstrates our dependability and reliability on Him. It brings glory to God. You probably have heard this quote from John Wesley, "God does nothing except in response to our prayer." Therefore, if you are waiting but not praying, God has nothing to respond to.

In The Book of Acts of the Apostles, chapter 1, Jesus told the disciples to remain in Jerusalem and wait for the promise of the Father, which is the Holy Spirit: "And while being in their company and eating with them, He commanded them not to leave Jerusalem but to wait for what the Father had promised, of which [He said] you have heard Me speak" (Acts 1:4AMP).

If you read this passage in context you will notice Jesus is speaking of the Holy Spirit as the promise God the Father would send. The disciples heeded his command, but they weren't merely waiting. Instead, all one hundred and twenty souls of men and women maintained an attitude of praying while waiting for the promise. "All of these with their minds in full agreement *devoted themselves steadfastly to prayer,* [waiting together] with the women and Mary the mother of Jesus, and with His brothers" (Acts 1:14 AMP).

Notice the verse says they *"devoted themselves steadfastly to prayer"* while waiting. In chapter two of Acts, the promise was fulfilled as the Holy Spirit descended like fire on Pentecost. So if you are waiting on a promise, do so in steadfast prayer. Don't get tired of praying while waiting and don't give up. Receive grace to be steadfast in prayer in Jesus name.

As valuable as prayer is in general, how you pray is also very important to God. Chapter 11 of this book delves deeper into the *irresistible prayer* that touches God's heart.

THE EARLY DAYS OF OUR SCHOOL

Christian education for children and young people is at the heart of our ministry. Due to this, Lily and I founded Millennium Christian School under God's guidance and direction. It's a Christ centered school designed to raise Nehemiah's for Christ in Africa who will use their education to change Africa and the world for the better. Though we are still considered to be at the foundational stage of our establishment and have more work to do, more investment to make in order to reach our ultimate goal, we aren't where we were when we founded the school four years ago. In the early days of the school, we met with some unbearable challenges that I want to use to further emphasize the importance of actions and attitudes when waiting.

We started school in the summer of 2016 and had no students for the first two weeks. Parents came to inquire, but never came back for enrollment. We had to take initiative to phone those parents who left their numbers with us during their inquiry, but most replied saying they couldn't enroll their kids in a school where there were no other kids. Others complained of lack of money for tuition.

At that point, Lily and I reasoned we should let them enroll these kids and pay later. But when we made this move by phoning them to bring their kids for enrollment and let them pay later, they all disappointed us. None of them showed up. The first two weeks were like hell for us, but through God and the promises in His Word, we were able to find solace and courage to stay undisturbed, unperturbed and hopeful things would change for the better.

However, in those two weeks, we went to work at the school in the morning and closed in the afternoon at the exact time we close today. Throughout the empty day, we studied the Bible, and other related books, laughed, had fun, prayed together, went into the community, moving from house to house to share our school flyers with them. Suddenly, something different happened the next week! A lady came with two little girls to discuss the school with us, she told us she would come back and collect our phone number. A couple of days later, we didn't hear from her as promised but remained undisturbed. Then, one morning before school, the lady phoned telling us she still wanted to enroll her kids with us, but the money her husband was expecting hasn't come through yet. This very moment Lily and I knew the Lord had just given us students. We told her that if she really wanted to enroll the kids, then she could come without money for now until her husband got paid. This was how Millennium Christian School started, with two little girls. All through that term, they were the only students we had, but we were so thankful to God Almighty for this miraculous breakthrough.

The second term brought two other girls who had not gone to school for a long time. Once again, we enrolled them without payment, because their parents were also facing financial hardship. We needed students, and they needed school, so we offered them a scholarship. We continued our house to house outreach and praying. Several evenings each week, Lily and I walked street to street in the community praying and commanding the land to release students for our school and worshipers for our church. We closed our first school year with 12 students who didn't pay school fees. Today, four years later, we have over seventy students with only five students on our scholarship program.

God is so good and faithful. He never delays, disappoints or fails. Most of the miracles He will do in our lives, He performs through us because we are co-laborers with God. We have our role to play while waiting. We can't be passive while waiting for God. Faith requires action while we wait.

Seek the Lord to discover what you need to do while you are waiting for Him to move; then, do it. Do you remember what Mary, Jesus' mother, said at the marriage in Cana of Galilee when the host felt disappointed because the wine had run out halfway through the celebration? Mary said to the servants, "Whatsoever He says to you, do it". (John 2:5) Jesus' following instruction seemed simple: fill the water pots, then draw out the water and serve it. If the servants had been unwilling to fill the water pots or draw out the water to serve, no miracle would have occurred. There is work to do in the waiting of the miracle. Personalize Mary's instruction, "Whatsoever He says to you, do it," and apply it to your life while you are waiting.

WAITING IN DISOBEDIENCE

Believers must be willing to do God's will when waiting or He won't be able to fulfill His promises in our lives. Put it in another way, disobedient during your waiting season will cost you His promises. Disobedience simply means: *acting on your own terms or being your own authority and not submitting to God.*

King Solomon warns "...Walk in the ways of your heart and in the sight of your eyes; But know that for all these God will bring you into judgment." (Ecclesiastes 11:9) He never recommended doing whatever made a person feel happy, but instead warned us a lifestyle focused on self would lead to destruction. We can't do whatever we want, while claiming to be waiting on God. Instead, while you are waiting on God, you need to be obedient to what he has already directed you to do.

Therefore, Believers can't walk in unforgiveness, pride, hatred, strife, immorality, or worldliness while waiting for God's promises to manifest in our lives. This kind of living points to the unfaithful servant Jesus talked about in Luke 12:41–48. Jesus warned Believers to be faithful, ready, and watchful while waiting for His second coming. Peter asked the Lord, "Lord, do you speak this parable only to us, or to all people?" Luke 12:41.

Jesus' answer is clear. Yes, His message applies to all Believers: "And the Lord said, who then is that faithful and wise steward, whom his master will make ruler over his household, to give them their portion of food in due season? Blessed is that servant whom his master will find so doing when he comes...he will make him a ruler over all that he has" (Luke 12:42–43).

Notice, the master will reward the faithful servant at the right time that did his will during the waiting season. In other words, the faithful or the obedient servant will get the promise. But let's hear what Jesus said about the unfaithful or disobedient servant: "But if that servant say in his heart, My master is delaying his coming,' and begin to beat the male and female servants, and to eat and drink and be drunk" (Luke 12:45).

Did you notice the servant thought in his heart: *"My master is delaying his coming?"* His thoughts resulted in his oppressive and sinful lifestyle. This servant thought delays or waiting seasons were opportunities to follow his heart and do whatever he wanted, enjoying life on his own terms, instead of following His master's previous commands. This unfaithful servant believed he could live against the principles of God and still receive the promises or rewards. What he never knew was his period of waiting was a test of his heart. Time revealed the truth in his heart. He was not a faithful believer. Unfortunately, his conclusion was terrible. Jesus' next words are terrifying: "The master of that servant will come on a day when he is not looking for him, and at an hour when he is not aware, and will cut him in two and appoint him his portion with the unbelievers" Luke 12:46.

The word I want you to notice above is *"unbeliever."* This word answers Peter's question from verse 41, when he wanted to know who the Lord was directing the parable to, whether only Jesus' disciples or to everyone. Peter wanted to know if this parable was for Christians only or included non-Christians. Obviously, Jesus wasn't addressing unbelievers or non-Christians in this parable. Otherwise, He wouldn't have said this unfaithful servant would share the same fate as unbelievers. As a matter of fact, an unbeliever isn't a servant of the Lord. One must receive the gift of salvation to be a servant of the Lord. This parable is a warning for Believers (Christians) to remain faithful before the day of the Lord comes. Remember the five foolish virgins I discussed earlier, who didn't have enough oil to keep their lamp burning? That parable corresponds to this parable. The lack of oil represented their lack of faithfulness to the Lord.

The second lesson I want you to learn In Jesus' parable in Luke 12 is in verse 47: "And that servant, which knew his master's will, and did not prepare himself or do according to his will, shall be beaten with many stripes." Notice here the Lord is addressing Believers who knew what to do but never did it. They weren't ignorant of God's will. They were obstinate and willfully transgressed God's will. Jesus says, these Believers shall have more punishment than unbelievers or non-Christians. As Christians, Jesus' words should challenge us to create and maintain a reverential fear of God and cause us to remain faithful and obedient to His will, as we wait for the Lord Jesus to come again.

We should use delays, our waiting or testing seasons, as an opportunity to prepare ourselves to do God's will before the arrival of the promise. Use your suffering seasons to learn how to obey and stay faithful to God. That is exactly how Jesus learned to obey God's will; it was through his suffering and waiting season. The writer of Hebrews explains, "Though he was a Son, yet He learned obedience by the things which he suffered" (Hebrews 5: 8).

THE GREAT MARRIAGE

Individually, we all have something at this moment in this life we are waiting on or trusting God for fulfillment. It could be for a financial or business break-through, the return of a prodigal child, healing, or something else specifically. I have mine too. However, as Christians there is something more important that we are all waiting for together: the marriage supper of the Lamb. This will be the marriage between Jesus and the Church, which will take place at the end of this age. Every Christian from the first century till that great day in the future, both those living on earth and those living in God's presence, are all waiting for our great day. This great day is what the parable of the faithful and unfaithful servant in Luke was about. I want to take you a little deeper here on how we can actually wait faithfully and obediently for our great marriage.

The Bible calls this day our blessed hope. It's the one thing that distinguishes us as Christ's followers from the world. Sometimes, I just can't wait for this event to happen, because we are strangers on a pilgrimage in this world. Our hope is not in this world or what it will offer (1 Peter 2:11). Most believers all over the world share my excitement too. Honestly, it will be the sweetest thing ever in our Christian faith to be with Jesus for all of eternity. The thought that we shall be just like Him, even rule and reign with Him forever and ever is breathtaking! I want to encourage you not to take your mind from this glory that will be revealed in us one day. The early church set their minds on this promise, and it sustained them through extreme persecution and martyrdom.

Here is something else you must know. Satan wants to distract you away from this event so you will be as the unfaithful servant in Luke and lose your promise. The devil will do everything he can to achieve his goal. He will tempt you with money, pleasure, fame and power to buy your heart away from the blessed hope. Satan will try to make you focus on this world and how you feel right now in hope you will forget about the next one. Let me remind you about Heaven. This world is a mess compared to heaven. It is like comparing a filthy ghetto to Buckingham palace, but even my comparison falls short in depicting the glory of Heaven. There is nothing on earth or in this life worthy to desire or crave when compared to our Heavenly home and Christ Jesus!

Believers cannot fail to remember our ultimate destination and goal in Christ. We must not let the things of this world blind us to our future. And, we must maintain patiently for God's timing to bring our promised future to pass. This waiting season must be spent wisely. Believers have important tasks to complete before we reach Heaven. Primarily, God still needs us to shine our light on others, to show them God's love, so they too can receive the salvation God has offered the world through His only begotten Son, Jesus Christ. Like the apostle Jude puts it, "pulling them out of the fire", that is, Believers are to help pull the unsaved from the wrath of God that is coming into the glorious hope of Christ (see Jude 22-23).

God also desires Believers to use this waiting season before Christ's return to purify ourselves of every sinful lifestyle associated with our old nature. We are to completely put off the old man and be prepared as a bride fully ready for her bridegroom, without spot, wrinkle or blemish. The Bible tells us, this beautiful and prepared church is what our Lord Jesus Christ is coming to receive. Thus, God wants us to be at peace with ourselves and be without any reproach morally before His return. He wants Believers to be removed from living sinful lifestyles under the disguise of grace and not be like the ungodly men Jude wrote about (see Jude 4). For further growth and spiritual study, read the following Scriptures: Ephesians 5:27, 2 Peter 3:14, Revelation 19:7-8, 1 John 3:3, Heb. 12:14, 1 Peter 1:13-15, Philippians 2:14–15, 2 Corinthians 7:1, 1Thessalonians 5:23, Colossians 1:22, 2 Corinthians 11: 2, Jude 24.

The characteristics described in these verses for God's people include: *without spot, or wrinkle or blemish; faultless; pure; chaste and holy*. These attributes should not scare a Believer or seem unattainable. God has commanded them of us, so they are possible. At one point in my walk, the ideals scared me because they revealed my inabilities. I focused on my lack of these traits and not God's abilities to provide them. When I realized God was commanding me to reach these characteristics not on my own merits but by focusing on His abilities 2Corinthians 12:9, I started realizing God had already made me holy in Jesus. God had planted His seed of righteousness in me through Jesus and it would grow and produce the fruits or characteristics He desired. My obligation to the growth of this seed was important too. I need to nurture my new nature and water this seed by reading and reflecting on God's word daily. As I leaned on God and turned away from my old nature, God gave His seed inside my heart increase, and I grew more of God's desired traits.

I encourage you to never resist the work of God and His grace in your life. If you yield your will completely to it, God will produce the most beautiful traits within you. If you look up those scriptures above, you will notice one repeated phrase, **"*He will present you*"** faultless, without spot, and blameless. You aren't working all the work alone to be faultless or blameless. He not you does the presenting. God will do the purification and sanctifying work in you through His Holy Spirit. Everything about our eternal redemption from start to finish, that is, from the moment we receive Christ to the day we shall all appear in His presence is completely the work of God through His Holy Spirit indwelling us. Now, that doesn't mean we have no role to play in the refining process. Our role is to cooperate with God and yield our will completely to His grace.

CHAPTER 5

MOTIVATIONS

"I would have lost heart, unless I had believed that I would see the goodness of the Lord in the land of the living."
Psalms 27: 13

At the start of our ministry, God used a true life story shared by a prominent Nigerian pastor whom we looked up to as one of our spiritual fathers, to encourage Lily and I to fight against discouragement at all costs. As a result, we never gave up our ministry work no matter how tough things become.

The story was about a certain pastor of a local church, who God called to begin a new church in one community. He fasted, prayed and evangelized the entire community but couldn't get a harvest. Obviously, it seems as if the ground was iron, maybe rock hard. However, unknown to him, God was working out something that would cause a lot of people to relocate into that community. Regrettably, before God would finish what He was doing, this pastor got discouraged and quit his ministry. On the other hand, about the same time, another pastor started a ministry in the same community. The people God caused to relocate to this community, as a reward for the toiling and hard work of the pastor who quit, now became a harvest of the new pastor. He ended the story by saying, this new pastor must have concluded ministry was so easy, without knowing what really happened to the pastor before him.

I share this story to emphasize the importance of being patient as Christians, and how the lack of patience can cause us to lose our reward. This pastor was obedient to start his call and was diligent in how he prayed, fasted and performed his outreached. But sadly, he lacked the holding on or finishing power to stay through the difficult times. He started well but didn't finish well. The first pastor was strong and determined but lacked endurance, perseverance and patience. As a result, he forfeited his reward of a harvest to another. Hear what Jesus said about this kind of person: "For in this the saying is true: 'One sow another reaps'" (John 4:37). Jesus also said in the next verse something that applies to the latter pastor too: "I sent you to reap that for which you have not labored; others have labored, and you have entered into their labors."

The second pastor received a bounteous blessing fairly rapidly on the labor sowed by another. God can give us in a short time what we couldn't have accomplished in many years' time. If we choose to do God's will, we must wait for Him. That is exactly what happened to this new pastor. I believe God knew the second pastor's heart in the story was willing to obey Him to the finish line and so He favored him with the harvest of another.

Brother Lawrence, the Seventeenth Century French Monk put these words more succinctly: "That it was impossible, not only that God should deceive, but also that He should long let a soul suffer which is perfectly resigned to Him, and resolved to endure everything for His sake." This is so true. When we decide to love and obey God no matter what we face, God not only comes to help us, He also ensures we don't suffer any longer than necessary. Remember, that is what we discussed earlier in the section: The Strong Will Faint.

For instance, Jesus Christ, our perfect example, suffered before and during the cross but it wasn't more than absolutely necessary, because He had made up His mind, fully resigned and resolved to endure everything it would cost Him to bring His Father's will of salvation for the world. Knowing the bliss of the end result, our salvation, Jesus' suffering was reduced. Therefore, God not only helped Jesus in his time of suffering, He also ensured this wasn't longer than necessary for His beloved son. It is important to understand Jesus perfectly made up His mind and was fully resigned and resolved to endure everything God placed before Him. Let us read some of His words in the gospel of John: "Jesus said to them, 'my food is to do the will of Him who sent me, and to finish His work'" (John 4:34).

Did you hear that? Next let us look at Jesus' prayer at the garden of Gethsemane before facing the cross: "Saying, 'Father, if it is your will, take this cup away from Me; nevertheless not My will, but Yours, be done'" (Luke 22:42). It will interest you to know how the Father responded to that prayer. The next verse tells us immediately after Jesus prayed those words, the Father sent help to Him: "Then an angel appeared to Him from heaven strengthening Him" (Luke 22:43).

God will always strengthen and deliver everyone who has perfectly resigned his or her future to Him and resolved to endure everything for His sake. Also, Jesus Himself told His disciples (including you and me) the criteria for following Him, undertaking a divine calling or mission. He wanted us to count the cost before making up our minds to start anything for His sake: "Whoever does not persevere and carry his own cross and come after (follow) Me cannot be My disciple. For which of you, wishing to build a farm building, does not first sit down and calculate the cost [to see] whether he has sufficient means to finish it? Otherwise, when he has laid the foundation and is unable to complete [the building], all who see it will begin to mock and jeer at him, Saying, This man began to build and was not able (worth enough) to finish" (Luke 14:27 – 30 AMP).

Notice that it was finishing and not starting that was important to Jesus. It should be more important to you too, because what you start but fail to finish doesn't end with you. God will give your work to another person to finish, just like He did to that Nigerian pastor who labored hard and gave up so another enjoyed the fruits of his labor. King Solomon knew this principle firsthand, which is why he also wrote: "Finishing is better than starting" (Ecclesiastes 7:8 NLT).

Who are the finishers? They are those who count the cost then make up their minds, completely resigned to endure whatever comes their way. The finishers are the ones enabled from above to achieve their course successfully. With that in mind, you can see the first Nigerian pastor either didn't first count the cost or didn't make up his mind to endure whatever the costs were for the sake of the One whom he called Lord. He became discouraged and grew tired when delay happened.

Conversely, the opposite must be true of the new pastor. He wasn't lucky, neither was he favored above the first, as if God was more partial to him than the first. For God is partial to no man and His nature is revealed in Acts 10:34-35. Instead, he had counted the cost and was resolved to finish the work given to him. Therefore, God finished the work for him.

Now, the big question is what would make a person want to make up their mind to endure delays, disappointments and failures in order to finish or reach their ultimate goals? What motivates a person to pursue patience and persevere in the face of the unbearable?

The Longman Dictionary of Contemporary English defines the word motivation as *"motivation is the eagerness and willingness to do something without need to be told or forced to do it."* Secondly, it defines motivation as, *"the reason why you want to do something."*

When we take a conscientious look at the definitions of motivation, we understand people can't do something difficult on their own without first being motivated to do it. To wait patiently for long periods of time hoping something good happens in our lives in the midst of disappointments and failures is not our human nature. In other words, we can only pursue and practice patience if we are motivated.

What are the reasons Christians have to stay motivated and walk in patience? There are four reasons I have identified from personal experience and God's Word. They are

1. **God's goodness**
2. **God's faithfulness**
3. **God's wisdom**
4. **Our Love for God**

The first three reasons are the objects of our hope and trust. As such, I refer to them as the organs of patience. These organs are essential to the work of patience. However, of the four reasons for our motivation to follow through, our love for God is the highest form of motivation.

God's Goodness

The first reason why people want to be patient in times of delays, disappointment and failure is God's goodness. God's goodness is a core attribute and nature of God distinguishing Him from man and His other creatures. God's goodness means God's love, kindness, graciousness, compassion, and mercy. He not only contains all these attributes but bestows them on people even when we don't deserve them. It's God's goodness that makes God understand our needs, feel our pain, and causes Him to reach out to us to rescue us from our distress. This is why it is impossible for God to forsake or abandon us in our seasons of trial and suffering. The following scriptures points to this truth: Genesis 28:15, Deuteronomy 31:6, 1Chronicles 28:20, Joshua 1:5, Psalms 37:25, Isaiah 49:14-16, Matthew 6:25, 34, Matthew 28: 20, Hebrew 13:5.

The goodness of God makes it impossible for God to forsake or fail His children when they face trials or suffering, especially for the sake of His name. When we become grounded and rooted in this understanding of how good, loving and caring God is, it will motivate us to endure and persevere in faith through our moments of darkness. We know

God won't forget us. We have to hope and trust God for His goodness because He can never fail, forsake or forget us. On the contrary, if we fail to hope and trust God's sovereign love, care and goodness for us when our faith is being tried, we wouldn't be able to endure hardship as soldiers of Christ. Instead, we will become weary, bitter, and give up in the process. The Psalmist affirms this truth: "I would have lost heart, unless I had believed that I would see the goodness of the Lord in the land of the living"(Psalms 27:13). Did you notice what David said kept him from giving up? It was his hope and trust in God's goodness. WOW! This is the same David that said in Psalms 37:25: "I have been young, and now am old; yet I have not seen the righteous forsaken."

God's goodness will never allow Him to forsake His children, not for a split second. In one of the scriptures I quoted above, Isaiah 49:14-16, God says even though a mother in all her affection for her sucking child may possibly forget that child, He would NEVER forget us. God also tells us in Isaiah that our names are carved into His hands. Every time God looks at the scars on Jesus' hands, He sees your name carved there. He can never forget you and how important you are to Him. It was this belief that David had about God that helped him hold on and kept him from giving up. It also gave him the courage to wait on the LORD until the end: "Wait on the LORD; Be of good courage, And He shall strengthen your heart; Wait, I say, on the LORD!"(Psalms 27:14).

Amazingly, the goodness of God is for all people, including the saved and the unsaved souls. The earth is full of the goodness of the Lord, not only on the side of the righteous. Psalms 145:8-9 tells us, "The LORD is gracious and full of compassion, Slow to anger and great in mercy, The LORD is good to all, And His tender mercies are over all His works."

Did you notice the verse 9? It says, *"the LORD is good to ALL,* and His tender mercies *are over all His works"* not some. The whole world, not just Christians can access God's goodness. However, while His goodness towards us that are saved is to motivate us to hope and trust Him in times of hardship and suffering, it is also towards the unsaved to motivate them to repentance. This is what the Lord conveys to Nicodemus in John 3:16. The essence of God's love perfectly demonstrated on the cross is to bring all who will believe to repentance and salvation in Christ Jesus. Paul also confirms this in Romans 2:4, "Or do you despise the riches of His goodness, forbearance, and long suffering, not knowing that the goodness of God leads you to repentance?"

The apostle Peter also said the reason God is patient towards us, that is, waiting patiently for people during this horrible time on earth is because of His goodness and love for unbelievers, "…not willing that any should perish, but that all should come to repentance" (2Peter 3:9 KJV). Sadly, the window of time for His goodness leading to repentance will not always be open forever. In fact, it will close, and the Son of God shall return in His glory to take His bride. Faithful Believers will be with Him forever. James wrote: "for the coming of the Lord is at hand, *You also be patient,* Establish your hearts, for the coming of the Lord is at hand" (James 5:8).

I encourage you to hope and trust in God's goodness if you are facing any distress right now, but heed this warning of repentance if you're not truly saved. If your season of waiting has shown you an unrepentant and bitter heart toward God, and you want to give your life completely over to Him and have true salvation, kindly turn to the last page of this book where you will find a prayer just for you.

GOD'S FAITHFULNESS

The word *faithfulness* and *faith* are translated as the same word in Hebrew. The Hebrew word is **Emunah**, meaning firmness. *The International Standard Bible Encyclopedia* elaborates the meaning of faithfulness further: *"faithfulness denotes the firmness, constancy, and unchangeableness of God in His relations with men, especially with His people."* According to the *New Strong's Exhaustive Concordance of the Bible,* other words for "emunah" are *"fidelity, steady, truly, and truth."* When people possess the characteristics of firmness or faithfulness, it means they won't change their words, actions, or nature based on what happens. In other words, they can be trusted and depended upon. This is what true faithfulness or to be faithful is really all about. No human being apart from God possesses this attribute in entirety. The nature of God's faithfulness can only begin to flow into us as we draw nearer to Him in our everyday life. King David continually praised God's Faithfulness so much in His psalms. Here are some of them: Psalms 36:5, 40:10, 89:1-2, 5, 8, 24, 33, 92:2, 119:90, 86, 138.

In Psalm 138:2, God said He magnified His word above His name. WOW! He is a God of integrity. You can hold or accuse Him by His word, and surely He will still stand by it. The prophet Isaiah in prophesying about the Messiah, describes the belt of His waist as faithfulness (see Isaiah 11:5), which Paul also called the belt of truth when listing our spiritual weapons (see Ephesians 6:14). Jeremiah describes the magnitude of God's faithfulness as great (see Lamentation 3:23), meaning, it was plenteous and sufficient. God's faithfulness has no limit.

Titus 1:2 and Hebrews 6:18 said, "it is impossible for God to lie." In other words, it is impossible for God to be unfaithful. Time and space will not permit me to list all the scriptures affirming the truth about God's faithfulness. However, I want to reiterate here you can hope, trust, depend and rely on God even in a fiery furnace or in the lion's den. God will surely come through for you. When God gives you His word, no matter the delay or failure you face fret not, because God never changes his Word (2 Corinthians 1:20). "Forever, O LORD. Your word is settled in heaven. Your faithfulness endures to all generations" (Psalm 119:89-90). God's word will surely come to pass. David said in Psalm 119:31 saying, "I have bet my life on your Word. Don't disappoint me."

God's faithfulness was one aspect of God King Saul never knew. Saul forfeited his kingdom for another who knew this firsthand. As you know, by God's Word from the prophet Samuel, King Saul was instructed to wait in Gilgal for seven days, which he did but couldn't wait for the one who commanded it to arrive. If Saul knew God never changed His word, he would not only have waited the seven days, but he would have waited for the one who said he was coming to make the sacrifice on Saul's behalf to bless him.

Think about Abraham, who in all hopelessness that surrounded him and Sarah, never doubted God's faithfulness. Hear his testimony: "And not being weak in faith, he did not consider his own body, already dead (since he was about a hundred years old), and the deadness of Sarah's womb. He did not waver at the promise of God through unbelief, but was strengthened in faith, giving glory to God, and being fully convinced that what He had promised He was also able to perform"(Romans 4:19-21).

This is the kind of faith that moves God's hand for our favor. Keep this in your heart: any promise God has given you in secret, He will perform in the open. No delay, disappointment, or failure you're going through will stop His word from being accomplished. Hold tight. In fact, go and rest for God will fulfill what He promised you (1 Thessalonians 5:24). God never changes His Word. His integrity is at stake, or else we could not trust Him.

God's Wisdom

The third reason to motivate us to wait patiently is God's wisdom. God is omniscience, which means He is all knowing and His wisdom is perfect, without mistake. God never makes mistakes. His wisdom is mighty and powerful. He knows what is in the dark. He sees the other side of life we don't see. His wisdom is Wonderful, and it's amazing when you get to know what He knows about you and your situation (Psalm 139:6). God's wisdom is beyond our comprehension and you may not understand most of the things He's doing in your life right now or why He's doing them. All you have to do is trust Him, that He knows what He is doing concerning your circumstances and what He is doing is for your good. There are times in our ministry when we really needed some things badly, but thank goodness we never got them at that time, because it later turned out the time we had them was always the best time. Perhaps, you have experienced something similar.

The resurrection of Lazarus is a perfect example of God's wisdom for timing. The Lord Jesus demonstrated the wisdom of God when He came two days after Lazarus was already dead, buried and stinking. Jesus had been notified earlier by Mary and Martha before Lazarus died to come as he was very sick. Yet, He purposely stayed back for another two days because He wanted to teach them and us that God is never too late. Everything God does is perfect and at the right time (see John 11:1-44).

God's wisdom is awesome and perfect. He wants us to trust His wisdom because He has put every purpose in our lives for a perfect time and season (Ecclesiastes 3:1). God knows when things will be good and favorable for us and when they will not. He is wiser than us and knows more than us. We must trust Him completely in times of delay, disappointment and failure, especially on how and when He will move in our lives and circumstances to help us. God knows our past, present and future. When we know this, it settles every doubt or question we have in our hearts concerning when He will bring or take things out of our lives. The scripture says: "He has made everything beautiful in its time" (Ecclesiastes 3:11).

Notice it's not in our time, but in its time, the time established by God. The thing you are trusting God for has a perfect time for it to manifest. You can only enjoy it when it manifests in the perfect time.

This should warn us when we push for things to happen in our time, they might come but the end will be ugly like with the prodigal son. Trust God knows the best time for you.

Our Love For God

Our love for God is the highest form of motivation in our pursuit of patience, especially when we are facing delays, disappointment and failure. Our love for God will motivate us to wait patiently on God more than understanding of His goodness, faithfulness and wisdom. This is because God never gives up on us. Instead, we are the ones who give up on Him. God said twenty-six times in Psalm 136, "His mercy endures forever." God's love for us never fails.

The Message translation renders it this way, "His love never quits," and verse 23 tells us, "Who [God] remembers us in our lowly state" (MSG). God's love compels Him to come after us like a man chasing after the woman he loves, to pick us up from the valley, but most times we have already walked away when He comes. Remember the first Nigerian pastor who planted a church in that community. God never gave up on him, rather it was him who gave up on God by not being able to wait on God's timing. I love the way Abraham Lincoln put it, "sir, my concern is not whether God is on our side; my greatest concern is to be on God's side, for God is always right." In other words, if there is ever a fault, it is never from God but from us.

Our love for God is what makes it possible for us to perfectly be resigned to Him and resolved to endure anything for His sake. To love God is to trust and obey Him. It is our love for God that makes us accept His will and trust His goodness, faithfulness, and wisdom to the end. God will always come to rescue and deliver us, but the question is will we patiently wait until He comes. Or will we be like the first Nigerian pastor who left and quit before God showed up mightily?

When people can't wait for God, it's either they are ignorant about God's love, faithfulness and wisdom, or they have a lack of love for Him. In most cases, it's usually a lack of love on our part. If we truly love God, we will be patient, bearing whatever attack comes, knowing God will carry us through it. Love is a matter of choice. We must choose to never give up. Paul defines love in 1 Corinthians, chapter 13: "Love endures long and is patient and kind;...Love bears up under anything and everything that comes, is ever ready to believe the best of every person, it hopes are fadeless under all circumstances, and it endures everything [without weakening]. Love never fails [never fades out or becomes obsolete or comes to an obsolete end."(AMP)

The characteristics of love characterized above express love is not what we feel or confess but is a product of our actions and behaviors (1 John 3:18). Love is an act of our will which manifests in our actions. If we employ this attitude of love expressed in the scripture and behave towards God with these willful choices, we will never give up on Him no matter how long it takes God to come through for us. This is the kind of love God has for us. It is also the same type of love God wants His children to seek and grow in because it makes us rooted, grounded and unshakably secured in the face of tribulations.

Do you recall the story of Jacob in chapter two of this book? His love for Rachel made him overlook fourteen years of hardship and waiting. It made him count that time as nothing to be with his sweet bride. If a man can do that for a woman he loves, how much more can you overlook while waiting for God?

My Encounter

There was a time I became worried about the numerical growth of our church. Then one day in my study hour, the Lord corrected me. Here is what He said to me, "Son, if souls, numbers, and other godly ministry pursuit is your highest goal, then you will still give up on Me one day when you don't see them. Worse, you can have them and be distracted. But if your highest goal is ME, knowing ME intimately, then no matter your ministry results, you will still be a very satisfied and fulfilled man, because you have lost nothing. Instead, you have gained everything, that is, ME. So listen son, I'm using these dry years to shake and set your priorities right, helping you to put first things first. Remember my words to the church of Ephesus" (Revelation 2:1–4). They were great and fruitful at everything except in their first love (ME), the very thing that matters most. I don't want you to go like others have gone. You are precious to Me."

Those words, like King Solomon said, became life to my soul and grace to my neck from that day. I hope and pray they have the same impact on you as you read them. Now let me ask you, what is your highest goal in life? If it is to know the Lord Jesus intimately and walk perfectly before Him, then I am excited to tell you that your priorities are properly set. Like Paul says, your heart is fully set on the things above (Colossians 3:1-2). I believe this was what the Lord wanted to first do for that Nigerian pastor who quit his ministry work too soon. God wanted to help set his priorities right. It was what Jesus did to the seventy disciples when they returned rejoicing because they had a fruitful evangelistic work. In their own words, "even the devils are subject unto us through your name" (Luke 10:17). Jesus was pleased with them, but his reply to them unveils to us what is foremost in His heart: "Nevertheless do not rejoice in this, that the spirits are subject to you, but rather rejoice because your names are written in heaven" Luke 10:20.

In other words, Jesus is saying, "fix your eyes on the things above, the big picture and don't let your joy and motivation be on things done here on earth, because that is the only way you cannot be distracted by the enemy and the worldly system we live in." If Jesus is your anchor or highest goal, you will always remain in His presence no matter the storm or wind that comes against you. You will always prevail against any challenge if you truly love Jesus. Be challenged to make Jesus the highest goal in your life. If you do so, your soul will always be in perfect peace.

CHAPTER 6

THE TRIMESTERS OF PATIENCE

"And I will pray the Father, and He will give you another Helper, that He may abide with you forever."
John 14:16

Patience is hard to develop and to maintain. It is simply because it grows only in soils of trials and tribulation like delays, disappointments and failures. This is the main reason why many Christians lack this admirable quality and don't want to pursue it. Unfortunately, the lack of patience has resulted in many troubles in our relationships, homes, health and our entire global culture.

Let me briefly share a story that Lily told me about a man with whom she does some of our school outsourcing work. It happened that before this man went into private business, he worked with a big firm. At some point, something came up in his workplace that really upset him and caused him to resign from his job. After a while he began to regret his action, but by the time he went back to tenderly apologize to his superior, he was told it was too late. They could not give him back his job. He said that event taught him to be a more patient person. Sadly, he learned it in a very hard way.

Unfortunately, there are many like this man in our world today. The rates at which relationships are tearing apart, homes and marriages are breaking, the health of people are failing, and morality is declining are very alarming. Even many who are supposed to finish well in their Christian race are cheaply giving in to obstacles that are not insurmountable and giving in to temptations that are completely resistible. The Bible tells us the last days will be characterized by great trials and persecution. Only patient, enduring Christians will survive this age (Matthew 10:22, Revelation 3:10). This warning should signal to us that we need patience today more than in any generation in history, especially if we are already in the pre-tribulation days and only the patient will survive.

Experience has shown many who desire patience either hate or are afraid of the process before this sweet fruit is produced in their lives. The fear of patience's process has hindered many Believers from taking the steps in developing this admirable fruit. Though nothing good comes easy, we must not forget that nothing about our Christian faith is ever earned. Everything in our Christian life is all about grace. This means not by the works we have done or will do can we acquire patience. From salvation to our daily walk with God and bearing Christian fruit, it is the work of God's grace, that is, divine enablement not by our effort that brings results. Scriptures clearly and strongly affirm this truth: John 15:5, 1 Corinthians 15:10, Philippians 4:13, Zechariah 4:6 and 1 Samuel 2:9.

However, like I said before, all that God requires from us is our cooperation through total submission of our will to His will and authority. Even our Lord Jesus who once lived and walked on this earth knew we could not make it on our own, which is why He said, "I will ask the Father, and He will give you another Helper." Jesus knew we needed help and continued in the sixteenth chapter of John verse 7. "Nevertheless I tell you the Truth; It is to your advantage that I got away; for if I go not away, the Helper will not come to you; but if I depart, I will send him unto you."

If Jesus said He must go to heaven so we can have the Helper, does that not demonstrate to us the significance of this Helper and the work He's going to be doing in our lives? The Helper's assignment touches every aspect of our being. He wants to help us in our day to day life. The good news is this Helper is limitless. He can be anywhere at any time and can reach and help as many people that invite Him all at the same time. Conversely, our savior Jesus while on earth couldn't do that because Jesus was limited by His human body even though He was fully God on the earth, He was also fully human when He was here. It meant He could not be in Israel, Africa, Europe, Asia, Australia, South American or North America simultaneously, but the Helper can. The Helper can help everyone, all the time, and everywhere. This is one of the reasons why Jesus said it was to our advantage that He goes away and sends the Helper.

But who is this Helper that bears such significance like this? Why should we look to the Helper for developing our patience?

Who Is The Helper?

To find out who this Helper is let us first look at the phrase, "another Helper" used by Jesus in John 14:16. The Greek word for "another" is "allon." Allon means another of same kind. This means whoever this Helper is, the Helper is just like our Lord Jesus Christ. The Helper is of the same kind, the same spirit, the same intent, the same substance as Jesus. In John chapter16, verse 26 Jesus fully unveiled the identity of this Helper: "But the Helper, the Holy Spirit whom the Father will send in My name." Notice the Holy Spirit is the Helper whom the Father sends at Jesus' request to help everyone who believes in and loves Jesus Christ. The Holy Spirit is not merely a messenger in the sense some people want to think, because Jesus said, "I will send Him to you."

The Helper is The Holy Spirit. The Holy Spirit is God, the third person in the Godhead, co-equal and co-eternal with The Father and the Son. This means the Helper possesses equally the divine essence or nature of God (Omniscience, Omnipotent and Omnipresence). Although they are one and equal in Glory, Majesty and Power, their functions are different. The Holy Spirit, our Helper, is the immanent presence and activity of God in the earth. The Helper carries out God's agenda and work on the earth, including helping Believers bear godly fruit, grow and mature to be more like Christ in their everyday lives. God is called the "God of Patience", then the Holy Spirit, our Helper is the Spirit of Patience (see Galatians 5:22). This means God the Holy Spirit is the source of patience and also the Helper we need to develop patience in us through our trials and tribulations.

Knowing God has provided us the divine help needed to develop patience through the person of the Holy Spirit, we should be encouraged. We are not alone in our battle against darkness. Our Helper is not solely with us to bring us out of the battle victoriously but also wants to use these battlegrounds as an opportunity to bear wonderful fruit in us to make our faith mature and stable.

Developing Patience

To develop means "to grow or change into something bigger, stronger, more advanced or more visible." This definition conveys an idea that for something to develop, it must evolve or sprout from something much smaller. Sometimes, it could even be from something not visible to the human eye. This is to say, every Believer has a measure of patience within us. It's a seed of patience indwelt in us by the presence of our Holy Helper living in us from the moment of salvation.

For instance, let's consider the development of a human life. Medical science says life begins at conception. A developing baby is called an embryo at the moment of conception. During this early stage of development, the embryo remains unseen to the physical eye. It will undergo three major stages of pregnancy development, called trimesters, before labor and delivery bring forth a baby. In each trimester, distinct changes occur that lead to the full development of the final baby. For example, the formation of major organs and body parts increase the baby's weight and size. Then finally, at labor and delivery, the fully formed baby is born. It's at this stage our physical eyes can see a baby and our hands can also touch and feel the baby.

Similarly, this is how patience is developed in us by the help of the Holy Spirit. Patience begins in a Believer much the same way an embryo is conceived in a woman and undergoes different stages of growth. This is why James wrote: "But let patience have its perfect work" (James 1:4). The Greek word for *perfect* here is *teleios* meaning *to be complete in growth or in mental and moral character*. In other words, **patience undergoes stages of growth before it becomes complete or be fully mature** in a Believer. I have identified four different stages for the growth of patience, which I termed the Word Trimester, Heart Trimester, Hope Trimester and the Trial and Delivery. Let's dive into them deeper.

THE WORD TRIMESTER

Every work of God begins in God's Word, or in a seed stage, including patience. Tertullian said, **"the entire fruit is already present in the seed."** The seed he was referring to was the seed of Christ, that is, the Holy Spirit, which comes to dwell in Believers when we believe and receive the Word of God. Patience is an outgrowth of God's Spirit (Galatians 5:22). Therefore, as Believers in Christ, we have the seed of patience in us already. Since the Word is a seed, we can rightly say, God's Word is the embryo of patience or the seed of patience.

However, this seed of patience in us needs nourishment to grow the same way a human embryo in a woman's uterus needs proper nourishment to advance to the next stage of development. God's Word is also the spiritual nourishment our seed of patience needs to grow into the next stage of patience. For this to happen, we have to allow the Word to dwell in us richly (Colossians 3:16). This means, we need to study the scriptures until the Spirit and life in them permeates our spirit, soul and body. The kind of Bible study capable of producing this level of impartation involves reading, meditating, and praying over scriptures. If you lack mature patience, this is exactly what you should be doing with this book and the Holy Scriptures. I highly recommend you read at the Scriptures at least twice, not skimming the reading.

THE HEART TRIMESTER

At the second trimester of human pregnancy, all the functional organs and systems the unborn needs are fully developed. But this is only possible, if the embryo has been well nourished with the proper nutrients. Similarly, the Holy Spirit uses the Word we have studied out of pure love for God to impart and perfect the love of God in our hearts. It's this kind of heart that is secured in the love of God which enables the formation of the organs of patience: God's goodness, faithfulness and wisdom we have previously discussed.

These vital organs are our motivators for patience and the object of our hope and trust. That is why the apostle Paul prayed for the Thessalonians, "Now may the Lord direct your hearts into the love of God and *into the patience of Christ.*"(2 Thessalonians 3:5). When our hearts are secured in God's unchanging and abundant love, we are able to hope and trust the organs of patience which have been formed in us. Trusting in God's goodness, faithfulness, and wisdom will lead us to our next trimester, the Hope Trimester.

THE HOPE TRIMESTER

During the third trimester, the baby's brain and neuron development is active. The unborn child's organs are functional and active. At this stage, an embryo/baby is able to open its eyes and moves around a lot. The end of the pregnancy is near. The baby is getting ready to appear. The pregnant mother is so eager at this stage to see her baby face to face. Somehow, I believe the unborn baby shares this hope and eagerness too.

There are a lot of good things happening to both the baby and the mother at this stage. Although the baby has more growing to do, the "I can't wait to be born feelings" are overwhelming, on both ends, I think. This expectation of birth or completion is the perfect wording to describe the stage of Hope. Every pregnant woman is hopeful as she gets closer to her due date. This is exactly how Lily and I felt whenever Lily's pregnancy entered the final stage for our children. Hope is the confident expectation that the invisible is about to become visible. Everything has been formed in the invisible realm and is simply waiting for that moment it will break through into the visible. Hope is that joyful period of waiting, knowing it is complete.

Similarly, the seed of patience is completely formed in the third trimester of hope. It is finally ready to be delivered through trial. In other words, hope is patience completed yet unborn. This is because hope paves the way for mature patience, and it is this hope that empowers us to trust in God's goodness, faithfulness and wisdom as we await our promise to be fulfilled. When hope arises, patience is due. That is why Romans 8:25 tells us, *"...if we hope for what we do not see, we eagerly wait for it with patience."*

However, this stage also comes with both physical and emotional challenges, because labor and delivery are near. Likewise, as we approach the trial and delivery stage, things often become more difficult or worse. Real hope disregards any negative emotions and presses ahead to delivery.

TRIAL AND DELIVERY

This is the big day nobody actually desires because of the seemingly unbearable pain it poses. A doctor once told me labor pain is the greatest pain in life. This is also true of the Christian trial and suffering. It is one of the greatest pains in the Christian life.

Even our Lord Jesus said the moment before his trial asked "if it is possible let this cup pass from Me" (Matthew 26:39). Why did He ask the Father to skip over the next part of His walk? One reason I believe is because of the severity of the pain and suffering both physically and emotionally that was ahead of Him. Unfortunately, like Jesus, our trials are unavoidable, but they are good for our faith. They help to refine, strengthen, and stabilize our faith. How we respond to the difficult seasons determines whether we will profit from them or not. This is what the apostle James taught and encouraged early believers: "My brethren, count it all joy when you fall into various trials" James 1: 2.

This means we should be joyful in a trial because it gives us an opportunity to gain patience (James 1:3). We don't often feel joy as the natural response to a painful trial, but knowing the trial is for our benefit and blessing can give us wisdom and help us to choose joy instead of focusing on only the pain. Patience is the virtue that stabilizes our faith during our waiting and trial season until we receive the promise. But this doesn't mean that trial in itself produces patience. Otherwise, think about the people you probably know that have faced various trials, yet still lack patience. Perhaps, that may describe you right now. Maybe you've endured trials but haven't learned patience. What it does mean is that trial is the means for developing patience the same way labor is the means to delivering a baby. How does our trial act as a means to produce patience in us? James continues: **"But let patience have its perfect work,** that you may be perfect and complete, lacking nothing" (James 1:4).

I have highlighted the phrase **"But let patience have its perfect work"** to answer two important questions. The first question is who is to let patience have its perfect work? We are the ones who need to let patience have its work, not the Holy Spirit. If we read that passage in context, we will find out James was writing to New Testaments Believers (James 1:2) including you and me. We are the ones to let or allow the work of patience to be completed in us during our trials, not the Helper. Whether or not patience is brought to a complete work is purely our responsibility.

The way we respond to our trials determines if the work of patience started in us from the seed stage will ever be completed or not. It's like a pregnant woman. She must be the one to do the pushing in labor, not the midwife. The midwife is her helper the same way the Holy Spirit is our Helper. However, the soon-to-be mother must do whatever the midwife tells her to do. She must obey or humble herself under the midwife. The anxious mother must not push until she's told, and once told, she must push with all her might.

This brings us to the second question, how do we let patience have its complete work? We allow patience to have its complete work by remaining under God's authority; that is, by submitting our will to God's Spirit and doing whatever is God's will for us. Simply put, it means to obey the Holy Spirit completely and even our obedience is the work of His grace as we depend on Him.

It is at the moment of our submission to God's authority that the ability to endure is borne in us the same way the woman who obeys the midwife gains the skills to be able to push out her baby successfully. A typical example is the trial of our Lord Jesus Christ.

THE EXAMPLE OF JESUS CHRIST

The way the Lord Jesus faced His trial before and during the cross is a perfect example for us to follow. The writer of Hebrews wrote, "who for the joy that was set before Him endured the cross" (Hebrews 12:2). Most readers would initially think that passage meant it was Jesus' hope alone in the glory ahead of Him that empowered Him to endure the suffering and death of the cross. Don't get me wrong, Jesus' hope was a great motivation, but His obedience was the key to His success.

Jesus knew He would be exalted to sit at the right hand of the throne of God after the cross. If He knew and had this hope all along, even before He started His earthly ministry, why did He pray three times in the garden of Gethsemane, repeating the same words in prayer to the Father, "If it is possible, let this cup pass from Me?" (see Matthew 26:36-44). Jesus needed divine strength to face His unbearable, the cross.

The Bible tells us Jesus was exceedingly sorrowful and heavy in agony, describing the magnitude of the pain He knew He would have to undergo to bring us eternal salvation. It would take divine power to bear or endure His trial perfectly. This power doesn't just come because we have hope in God's promises or because we know what we will enjoy tomorrow. Remember the Nigerian pastor who quit his ministry work most definitely had a promise from God too? He began with a hope. But when things became unbearable, he gave up his hope. Anybody can give up his hope if he has no sincere love for God, expressed in absolute obedience to His will. The power to bear the unbearable comes on us due to our obedience to God's will. When we submit to God's will and authority, He gives us grace (divine empower) to face and endure any trial.

Admittedly, in the development of patience, hope is a great motivation, but obedience or love for God is everything. That is why the moment Jesus submitted to God's will, despite the severity of pain He was to face, God gave Him strength to endure the cross. The Gospel of Luke reveals that truth, "Then an angel appeared to Him from heaven, strengthening Him" (Luke 22:43). The strength He gained was not to fight the Roman soldiers, but to endure scourging and the cross. This supernatural strength is the power to endure trial. It is birthed in us by the Holy Spirit through our submission and obedience to suffer for Christ. This is the nature of patience.

Patience now formed in you by God's grace, comes rushing out through trial into your season of acceleration, appointment and victory.

TRIMESTERS OF PATIENCE

1. The Word Trimester
God's word within us is planted.

2. The Heart Trimester
God's word is nourished in us through study, prayer, and trust.

3. The Hope Trimester
Confident expectation of God's word builds in our heart.

Labor & Delivery of Patience
Trials refine and strengthen our faith in God's word as His promises are manifest through the difficulties.

CHAPTER 7

7 LIES WE CANNOT BELIEVE

"He was a murderer from the beginning, and does not stand in the truth, because there is no truth in him. When he speaks a lie, he speaks from his own resources, for he is a liar and the father of it."
John 8: 44

Lie is Satan's greatest prowess in attacking the minds of God's people. He is lethal at it. The devil's mission on earth is to lie to the world, so they can rebel against God and His Christ. Lying was the first thing Satan did when he was sent down to earth (see Genesis 3:1-6), and the Bible tells us it will be the last thing he does on earth before being banish to the Lake of Fire for eternal destruction (see Revelation 20:7, 8, 10).

In John 8:44 Jesus exposed Satan, "He [Satan]...doesn't stand in the truth, because there is no truth in him." Satan has no ability to speak truth, even if he so wishes. But, of course we know, he doesn't. Furthermore, Jesus told us why the devil can't speak truth, nor does he possess the ability to do so. Jesus said it's because "he is a liar." I want you to know that isn't just his name or title. It's who he is, his very nature. The devil is a lie personified (he cannot change because his essence is a lie). Satan is the incarnate of lie and is the opposite of Christ, who is the incarnate Truth.

That's not all though, Jesus also called Satan the "father" of lies. That means the devil is the head and the highest authority in the act of lying or deception. In fact, Satan is the founder of every lie, and no creature on earth has ever lied like him or even came close to Satan's ability to lie. The devil is the greatest of all liars because lies originate from him. Recall what Jesus said, "he speaks from his own resources." Did you hear that? Satan doesn't have to gather information from people or the situation like lawyers do before he can falsify evidence. Let's take for example if there is a sales chain and lies are the product being sold. The

82

devil would be the only manufacturer. Then he would also deliver his product to distributors. Then these distributors would sell the product to Satan's sales representatives. Nobody can sell a lie to Satan because he owns them already. He created every lie.

This should make us as Believers in Christ to be careful, watchful and spiritually sensitive so that we can be able to discern and counter the lies of the devil, especially in our waiting seasons. Satan tries to take advantage of our periods of delay, disappointment, and failure to lie to us about God's love and provision. Satan's lies are very sharp and accurate to our situation or behavior. Worse, his lies can seem very convincing. To deceive Believers, Satan presents his lies like the truth or mixes them with a little truth to get us to doubt God's word. However, if you know and believe God's word like you know basic arithmetic, you will be able to discern and counter Satan's lies. Knowing God's word takes time. This means only a mature Christian who is truly grounded and rooted in the Word and living under the influence of God's Spirit is able to discern and counter Satan's lies. Anyone else can fall victim.

Remember Adam and Eve were Satan's first victims. Since then, countless others have fallen victim. This shouldn't create fear in you, but rather a hunger and love for the truth. A hunger and love for God's Word, because it is the only thing able to set you free from Satan's lies and deception. The Bible warns Believers of Satan's lies that will come heavy against God's people in the last days. The only way to overcome it is to be firmly rooted in the Word of God, anchored by the love of God, and filled with His Spirit.

Unlike Adam, when Jesus was tempted by the devil (see Luke 4:1–13) He was able to discern and counter the lies of Satan. Jesus is God's Word (see John 1:1).The Bible tells us Jesus loves righteousness and hates lawlessness (see Hebrews 1:9). As Christians, we have been called to follow His example all time.

Now that you know how powerful the enemy's lies can be and how only those who love God's Word are equipped and empowered to discern and counter them, then let me expose Satan's seven lies Believers cannot afford to accept when waiting for a promise, miracle or a divine intervention from God. Satan's seven lies are intended to make us doubt and give up on God's promises during our waiting season. Don't be surprised if these even come from the mouth of people you least expect, like Christians. Even the Apostle Peter was used by Satan to try to lie to Jesus, but Jesus saw through Peter to the deceiver behind him and the lie (Matthew 16:23). The devil will masquerade through any available vessel irrespective of who they are or the position or title they possess.

The order is irrelevant for the listing of the lies. Believers may or may not encounter these lies all within the same season. Being warned of them, helps you be armed to counter them when they arise.

WE WON'T BE ABLE TO ENJOY IT

This is one of the lies the enemy tells us in our waiting season: if you continue waiting on God for the breakthrough you will be too old to enjoy it by the time it comes, if it comes at all. Have you been tempted with this lie before? Some years back, I was encouraging a Christian friend to be patient and continue to trust God for a financial miracle to pay off a beautiful property they bought. She wrote me back saying, "when will He do the miracle, is it when I'm old or probably when I'm eighty-five years when I won't be able to enjoy it?" Who planted that thought in my friend that she wouldn't be able to enjoy her promise even if it did come? The answer is simple: the devil.

Now hear the Word of God to counter Satan's lie: "He has made everything beautiful in its time" Ecclesiastes 3:11. In other words, things are only and truly enjoyable in the right time God set for them to happen. Anything we get outside of God's time; we won't truly be able to enjoy as we ought. When God gives you anything in His time, it comes with peace and joy, which are the true characteristics of godly enjoyment. For example, Abraham and Sarah were very old by the time, Isaac, the promised child was born. Abraham was one hundred years old and Sarah was ninety years old (Genesis 21:5, 17:17). Even at this advanced age, Abraham and Sarah were excited and joyful about the miracle. Sarah said, "God has made me to laugh, so that all that hear will laugh with me".

The "all that hear will laugh with me," includes Abraham of course. Think about how happy the couple was for such a miracle child after waiting for twenty-five years. But the devil will want to make you think that their happiness didn't last long because they were so old. Perhaps you think their joy lasted only a couple of years before they died, but the bible records a different ending. God gave them health, strength and long life to enjoy Isaac. Sarah died at one hundred and twenty-seven years old (Genesis 23:1), 37 years of enjoying her miracle child. WOW! Isaac was a full grown man when his mom died. How about Abraham?

Abraham died at age one hundred and seventy-five. The Bible says Abraham died in good health and full of strength and life (see Genesis 25:7–8). Abraham witnessed his son, Isaac, getting married and even having grandchildren for him, Esau and Jacob.

Consider Job who suffered so much loss but was willing to wait for the time it would take for things to turn around for him, staying faithful to God. The Bible says when God turned Job's captivity, he didn't just have a double of all he lost. The Bible says Job saw his children's children to the fourth generation and died at old age full of days (Job 42:16-17).

God is faithful to not only provide the promise but allow you to enjoy it as well. Patiently wait for God's timing and trust Him to give you health, strength, and life to enjoy the blessing whenever they come. The bible provides so many good examples of this truth: Moses, Joshua and Caleb, David, Hannah, Ruth, and so many more.

OTHERS ARE GETTING AHEAD

Many people when they are not married, having children, buying a house, starting their dream careers, or whatever often feel the pressure of this lie. The devil lures them by taking their eyes off of God and what He has planned for us to what is happening in the life of someone else. It's ungodly to compare yourself with anyone, in any form. This type of behavior leads only to envy or jealousy and other grave sins. Think about Cain with Abel or Joseph's brothers. Envy and jealousy moved them to commit unthinkable crimes after they compared themselves to their brother. James wrote: "For where envy and self-seeking exist, confusion and every evil thing are there" (James 3:16). Paul also warned the Corinthians church in his second letter: "But they, measuring themselves by themselves, and comparing themselves among themselves, are not wise" (2 Corinthians 10:12).

In other words, those who compare themselves to each other are not wise. That is a kind way of saying they are foolish. You won't want to be foolish. The best way to counter this lie is with Jesus' truth, "The last will be first, and the first last" (Matthew 20:16). In other words, those who are ahead of you today, won't always be ahead of you tomorrow.

In Matthew chapter twenty, Jesus shared a parable where He likened the kingdom of heaven as a householder who went out early in the morning to hire laborers into his vineyard. He decided to pay a penny for a day's work. The first group of workers he hired early in the morning agreed to his proposed wage. Those he hired at other hours of the day he didn't specify what they would earn, although in his heart he had decided to pay them a penny for their work too, even when they started at 9am, noon, and 5pm. Before I continue, I want you to imagine what was probably going on in the minds of the guys hired at 5pm. They probably looked at others who had a job earlier in the day and pitied themselves for not having a job. Maybe they wondered what was wrong with them that they weren't chosen earlier to go to work. Maybe you've felt that way, that you weren't chosen for such and such a thing. The Holy Spirit wants me to announce to you it's not over yet, stand by God. He will help you sooner than you expect.

At the last hour, in the last minute, the householder found them doing nothing and hired them too. At the end of the work day, the man lined everyone up to be paid. He began by paying the last guys he hired. He also gave everyone the same wage. By time the guys who'd labored all day for their wage stepped up to receive their wages, they felt cheated and complained because they labored longer and harder than those who'd come late in the day. The householder replied to those who were not satisfied with their pay: "Is it not lawful for me to do what I wish with my own things? Or is your eye evil because I am good?" (Matthew 20:15).

Recall our lesson about comparing oneself with others. This was the error these laborers made. They now envied those who once envy them. Here is the lesson for you, if you can wait patiently for God's right timing, some of the people you envy today will be the ones envying you when the table turns. That is why Jesus concluded his parable saying: "So the last shall be first, and the first last." (Matthew 20:16).

Therefore, do not worry because people are ahead of you today. It is their time to be where they are. Rejoice with them. Your time is coming soon, and hopefully they will rejoice with you. David wrote a psalm speaking directly to being tempted to compare ourselves and our deeds with others who seem to be thriving in the world, especially evil people: "Be still and rest in the Lord; wait for Him and patiently lean yourself upon Him; fret not yourself because of him who prospers in his way, because of the man who brings wicked devices to pass. Cease from anger and forsake wrath; fret not yourself—it tends only to evildoing. For evildoers shall be cut off, but those who wait and hope and look for the Lord [in the end] shall inherit the earth" (Psalms 37:7–11 AMP).

I hope you caught that? If not go over it again and again until it sinks and sticks with you. I advise you to read the entire Psalm 37 and 73. They will teach you why you should not compare yourself with others, especially people who you don't know for sure the source of their "good life." Satan will use what seems to be the worldly "good life" to lure you into evil or to compromise the standards of God in some way in your life.

PEOPLE ARE LAUGHING

This is one of the lies the enemy will tell you in your waiting season. Perhaps this is your experience right now. People are laughing or mocking you because of the delays, disappointments or failures you are experiencing in a particular area of your life. I understand your plight. I can feel your pain, because I've been there. Any mocking or laughing will only be for a short period of time. Haven't you heard the saying that "those who laugh last, laugh best." So don't let laughing or mocking stop you. Jesus, our perfect example, was mocked by the Roman soldiers, the Jewish people and their leaders both on his way to the cross and on it, hanging there in agony.

Likewise the chief priests also, mocking with the scribes and elders, said, "He saved others; Himself He cannot save. If He is the King of Israel, let Him now come down from the cross, and we will believe Him. He trusted in God; let Him deliver Him now if He will have Him; for He said, 'I am the Son of God.'" Even the robbers who were crucified with Him reviled Him with the same thing (Matthew 27:41 – 44).

Notice even one of the thieves crucified alongside mocked Jesus. So many mocked and laughed at Jesus on the cross. Christ in His awesome wisdom kept silent and cool. The Scriptures says, "As a sheep before its shearers is silent, so He opened not His mouth."(Isaiah 53:7).

Jesus kept quiet because He knew our salvation was not only near, it was at stake. If He had attempted to prove His mockers wrong for one minute, He would have aborted the predetermined plan of God to save the world from Satan and sin. Jesus was able to be silent because He knew He had the victory already. Believers need to learn this lesson too. We need to not allow the laughing or mocking of those around us to distract us from the glory God is revealing in us. We do not need to defend ourselves from their false accusations either. Allow God to correct them. Your battle isn't just your battle, it belongs to the Lord, "Thus saith the Lord unto you, Be not afraid nor dismayed by reason of this great multitude; for the battle is not yours, but God's" 1 Chronicles 20:15.

Remember, Solomon's thought on this matter: Also do not take to heart everything people say, lest you hear your servant cursing you (Ecclesiastes 7:21). "He who mocks the poor reproaches his Maker; he who is glad at calamity will not go unpunished" (Proverbs 17:5).

The wisest man who ever lived (aside from Jesus) told us not to take everything negative to heart. He also told us that anyone mocking the poor was mocking God, and it would not go well with that person. Those who rejoice over your troubles will not go unpunished. God is a God of justice. Relax and wait on the Lord. He will be your testimony in the end. You will have His promised victory.

IT WILL NEVER END

In your waiting season, the devil will say you're waiting endlessly because your circumstance will not end. I want you to know that whatever you're going through now is only a gateway to the promise. This time will end, just be patient, and don't allow the devil to feed your impatience.

Do you remember the Bible story about Ruth? Ruth was married to one of the two sons of Naomi and for ten years she was childless. As if that wasn't enough, her husband died leaving her a widow. Think about that for a moment. Then imagine how that could affect the faith of an average Christian woman today. Yet, in the midst of all these unsurmountable troubles, Ruth was unperturbed, undisturbed and cheerfully hopeful. Her attitude through her trial season demonstrated what true patience is all about. True patience is the ability to remain unperturbed, undisturbed, and hopeful while waiting for something positive to happen. This is the kind of patience God's rewards. At the end of Ruth's story, we read how God adorned Ruth with so much glory. She married a great man (Boaz) and became the great-grandmother of King David and a place in Jesus ancestry (see Matthew 1:5). Patience pays.

When overcoming this particular lie, it will help you to meditate on God's word:
- For surely there is a latter end [a future and a reward], and your hope and expectation shall not be cut off. (Proverbs 23:18AMP)

Your suffering is only for a specific period of time, not forever, and the end of your suffering will lead to great glory.
- But the God of all grace, who called us unto his eternal glory by Christ Jesus, after you have suffered a while, make you perfect, establish, strengthen, and settle you. (1Peter 5:10)
- For our light affliction, which is but for a moment, is working for us a far more exceeding and eternal weight of glory. (2 Corinthians 4:17)

Your joy is coming again after your season of suffering.
- For His anger is but for a moment; His favor is for life; weeping may endure for a night, but joy comes in the morning. (Psalm 30:5)

Your trial is not an end in itself, but a gateway to a good life.
- Who fed you in the wilderness with manna, which thy fathers did not know, that He might humble you, and that He might test you, to do you good in the end. (Deuteronomy 8:16)

IT ISN'T WORTH IT

This is another lie Satan is telling many Christians today. Yes, waiting can be difficult, but it has its rewards far exceeding an easy way out. Satan will tell you it isn't worth the stress, just give up. But remember, he is a liar. The victory you will have in the end is worth every moment of stress. Satan wants you to give up before you discover that truth. Think about Joseph. The victory he had at the end was even worth more than every moment of stress he went through.

The best way to counter this lie, as discussed in Chapter 6 of this book, is to rely on our Helper, The Holy Spirit to empower us. Within Believers dwells the power and presence of God. Through Him, we have the ability to overcome every difficult challenge or delay. Trusting in the Lord to help carry us through the situation will make the load lighter and easier. For scriptures to meditate on to overcome this lie, read: *1 Corinthians 15:10, Philippians 2:13, 4: 13, John 15:5, 1 Samuel 2:9, Zechariah 4:6 and Deuteronomy 8:16*. Trust God that He will carry you through your waiting season to your season of victory.

God's Timing Is Wrong

The devil will come in your season of waiting and plant thoughts like these in your mind: "don't you know God's time is too long and beside when do you think you will be due?" Sometimes these words will even come through the mouth of familiar people to persuade you to take short cuts or the fast lane. The sad fact is, I have seen many young people fall for this lie. The end is always ugly. There are no spiritual short cuts in life.

Truthfully, I cannot tell you that God's time is short or you will even get your promise soon, as defined by men. My father once told me, "God's time is usually long and not many people are willing to wait for it." He was so right. That is why many who follow Jesus end up compromising their integrity along the way. My father also said, "those who are able to wait are the ones you see people celebrate, because God will release His blessings on them without measure." The truths my dad shared with me came from his life experience as well as his knowledge as a Bible scholar.

His words are also supported by the apostle Peter, who wrote to the early Christians who were being mocked because they were waiting for the second coming of Christ: "But, beloved, do not forget this one thing, that with the Lord one day is as a thousand years, and a thousand years as one day" (2Peter 3:8).

If we are not careful, we could read this verse as God's time is very long, a day like a thousand years. But, if we read it another way, we can see that God can make what seems like impossible happen in just a day. When you make a choice to wait on God, He can give you in one day what will take you a thousand years to achieve. Why would God do that? It's because God sees one day of your waiting as one thousand years of waiting and is moved with compassion to help you.

Remember the story of our school I shared in chapter four? We closed our first school year with twelve students. When school reopened for the second school year, during the first week of resumption in one day the Lord added twenty new students to us without any advertisement or our usual home-to-home outreach. God! Notice I didn't say in one school year. In one day God gave us what we couldn't get in a year, that is, He did more in one day than we did the previous three hundred and sixty-five days through lots of labor. God rewards our patience. My brother and sister go and rest. Stop worrying yourself because God is working behind the scenes and when He's done, you will be amazed at how your life will change suddenly.

PATIENCE IS WEAK AND POWERLESS

The devil will tell us we shouldn't wait for God's judgment for those who mistreated or hurt us. Sometimes, Satan tells us forgiving those who offend us is a show of weakness and cowardice. In fact, the devil asks us why wait for God to get involved, when we could retaliate ourselves.

On the contrary, we know that God is a God of patience. God is not weak or powerless. In fact, the Bible tells us, He is the "Almighty God" and "All powerful God" (Genesis 17:1). That means God is full of power, and He never gets weak. God is also forgiving, yet there is swift and eternal justice to those who reject His mercy. God is never in a hurry, because He always has the victory. True power and patience are inseparable. That is why patience is called a virtue. The word virtue means power. Patience gives the owner power or control over his or her emotions, minds and will. Power to be proactive not reactive. Patience empowers us to be Christ-like: "Bless those who persecute you: bless, and do not curse. Rejoice with those who rejoice, and weep with those who weep. Be of the same mind toward one another. Do not set your mind on high things, but associate with the humble. Do not be wise in your own opinion. Repay no evil for evil. Have regard for good things in the sight of all men. If it be possible, as much as depends on you, live peaceably with all men" Romans (12:14-21).

It takes patience to accept these truths and choose to walk in them. As children of God, His characteristics become our characteristics as we yield to the Holy Spirit's work in our lives. The delays, disappointments, and failures we have faced were meant to refine God's characteristics in us until we conform to the image of Jesus.

7 Lies We Cannot Believe

1. We Won't Be Able to Enjoy It

2. Others Are Getting Ahead

3. People Are Laughing

4. It Will Never End

5. It Isn't Worth It

6. God's Timing Is Wrong

7. Patience Is Weak and Powerless

CHAPTER 8

DEALING WITH DISAPPOINTMENTS

"One thing I do, forgetting those things which are behind and reaching forward to those things which are ahead."
Philippians 3:13

To let go, forget or bury disappointments isn't an easy thing to do, especially if by nature you happen to be an emotional person. The truth is apart from God's Spirit helping us through the process, it's humanly impossible to completely forget and let go of painful memories. This is why many people who have been hurt in the past are still feeling effects of that pain today. The reason is because they haven't let it go completely or are not following the right guideline for forgiveness. So as emotional beings, the enemy takes advantage of our past pains, reminding us of negative feelings from the people or events that have hurt and wounded us.

These kinds of feelings, if allowed to grow, will only build strongholds for depression, bitterness, and anger stealing our peace and joy. Marinating in negative feelings also leads to cynicism, creating general distrust for good people in the future. The Bible tells us the enemy is a thief and he came to steal, kill and destroy, but the good news is that Jesus came to give back to us whatever the devil stole from us (see John 10:10). One of Jesus' missions is to heal the brokenhearted: "The spirit of the Lord is upon Me, Because He has anointed Me to preach the gospel to the poor, He has sent me to heal the brokenhearted" (Luke 4:18).

The brokenhearted are those who are grieving over the death of a loved one or over their own mistakes and sinfulness. Sometimes, the brokenhearted are grieving over the delay or non-fulfillment of their expectations. The list of reasons to be brokenhearted is long. But no matter what it is that you are grieving over I want to reassure you that Jesus came to heal you from grief irrespective of the pain or frustration they may be causing you. First, you have to give up your cause of grief completely to Jesus before the healing can begin. What you hold on to, will hold on to you. What you let go into Jesus' hand, will let you go (see Matthew 11:28, 1 Peter 5:7, Psalm 147:3).

Unfortunately this is where many Believers have failed. As a result of clinging to the grief that hurts them, they lose their peace and the opportunities the future holds for them. The ancient hymn, "What a Friend We Have in Jesus," captured it perfectly in its first stanza when it said, "O what peace we often forfeit, O what needless pain we bear, All because we do not carry everything to God in prayer." To put it differently, when we give our cares, burdens, brokenness and disappointments to God in prayer, in return He gives us peace, comfort, and new opportunities. Healing may not always come quickly; sometimes it takes time, and your patience will be required.

However, maybe you're saying in your heart, "But Brother Lawrence, you don't understand I've been wounded to my core. Are you saying God will restore my loss?" Yes, but maybe in a different way. Let's look into a time when a great king of Israel, David, was bereaved for his newborn. King David at a time in his life committed a despicable and exceptional sin in the sight of God when he committed adultery with Bathsheba, and later murdered her husband, Uriah, to cover-up his adulterous act. Later David grieved over his sin and repented when God rebuked him through the prophet Nathan. God in His great mercy and compassion restored David's salvation and fellowship (see Psalm 51), but the consequences of the sin still existed. Sin's consequences create godly fear and serve as an example of God's righteous judgment against sin, especially for spiritual leaders in all generations. God is merciful, but still judges sin today.

LETTING GO

In the case of David, one of the consequences of his sin was the death of the child conceived through his adulterous act. The prophet Nathan's pronounced on David, "because by this deed you have given great occasion to the enemies of the LORD to blaspheme, the child also who is born to you shall surely die" (2 Samuel 12:14). Notice Nathan said the child shall surely die, which means David cannot do anything to change it. God has already given His verdict. It is sealed, and there's no going back. Now, let us now examine David's attitude from the time the child became sick to when the child eventually died. The lessons Believers can learn from it will change our perspective about the death of loved ones.

Like every parent, David loved his newborn so much that when the child became sick as a result of God's judgment against him, David pleaded with God for the child via fasting and prayer, lying on the ground all night, even though the Lord had earlier told him about the fate of the child. David did nothing else but entreat the Lord for mercy for his son. Even when the elders of his house tried to get him to move or eat, he refused. David was grieved over the child as long as the child lived and fought in prayer to reverse the judgment of death. However, on the seventh day, the child died, confirming the Lord's promise of judgment. When the boy died, the servants were afraid to break the news to David, fearing his reaction. David perceived the child was dead and confronted them. They confirmed his suspicion. As soon as David knew of his child's death, straightaway he arose from the ground, cleaned up, anointed himself, changed his clothes. Then he went into the temple to worship God. He worshiped God!

I want you to notice David's reaction when the child was sick and died was totally unconventional. In fact, his servants were completely bewildered. They were still puzzling over what seemed like opposite behavior for a father, to mourn while the child is alive but sick, and to worship when the child was dead. Finally, they couldn't be silent in their confusion any more. They asked him in 2 Samuel 12:21 essentially, 'why did you fast and weep for your son when he was alive, but when he died you arose and ate food?"

David's reply contains a threefold lesson that can help Believers today: "And he said 'While the child was alive, I fasted and wept; for I said, who can tell whether the Lord will be gracious to me, that the child may live? But now he is dead; why should I fast? Can I bring him back again? I shall go to him, but he shall not return to me?'" (1Samuel 12:22-23).

Lesson #1: God is always gracious, but punishes the sins of His children. Unfortunately, David learned this in the hardest of ways.

Lesson #2: Do all God's Spirit enables you to do as long as the situation is still redeemable. But, after you have done all you can do, let it go.

Lesson #3: Your loved ones who die in Christ cannot return to you again, but thankfully you will meet them in Heaven and be with them forever. Praise God!

However, let me state here emphatically: our trying to hold on to something that is dead aggravates our pain, frustrations, and ultimately traps us in one spot longer than necessary. The concept of clinging to something death can apply to a multitude of things: people, animals, relationships, situations, failed dreams, etc. Unfortunately, this causes unnecessary trouble in our lives. Though David learned the cost of his sin, he was still able to accept God's will and moved on to his next season, where God gave him a beauty for his ashes.

BEAUTY FOR ASHES

God has given many awesome and wonderful promises in the Bible covering every aspect of our lives. I challenge you today to look them up and start confessing and receiving them into your life. However, for those who've suffered loss or disappointments of any kind, know there is a powerful promise: the Lord wants to give us beauty for ashes and double for our shame.

Isaiah 61:3 and 7 tells us, "To console those who mourn in Zion, to give them beauty for ashes. The oil of joy for mourning, the garment of praise for the spirit of heaviness; that they may be called trees of righteousness, the planting of the Lord, that He may be glorified… Instead of your shame you shall double honor, and instead of confusion they shall rejoice in their portion. Therefore in their land they shall possess double; everlasting joy shall be theirs."

Whenever the above scriptures cross your mind, I want you to think about people like Abraham, Joseph, Job, Naomi, Ruth, Jesus, the apostles, and every one of God's children you know who experienced a beauty for their ashes. Even more importantly, when you think of these scriptures, I want you to think about you. Yes, you! Why? Because that is exactly what the Lord wants to do in your life. What do the above scriptures really mean? They mean for your grief, shame, humiliation, delays, disappointments and failures or whatever else it is you have suffered because of your faith in Jesus, the Lord will give you something awesome, something far better than what you lost. God will give you something that will far exceed the value to what you lost. What God has planned for your good will stun your critics and humble your enemies.

But for this to happen, you have to let go of your ashes, shame or disappointment, taking them to Jesus. Let Him help you to heal. That was exactly how David acted before God gave him a beauty for the ashes of his lost child. Let's see the full story of II Samuel Chapter 12: "Then David comforted Bathsheba his wife and went in to her and lay with her. So she bore a son, and he calls his name Solomon. Now the Lord loved him (Solomon)" (2 Samuel 12:24).

Remember David went in after his child died and worshipped God. Then he moved forward. David never allowed the loss of his child to put him down forever in guilt and regret. Because he acknowledged the sovereignty of God and moved forward, he conceived another child. David called his new son's name, "Solomon." This is Solomon who became the wisest king in Bible history.

"Now the LORD loved him (Solomon)." In other words, God was saying, "I approve of this child." Through Solomon, God assured David of His forgiveness by sending the prophet Nathan again to David. Remember the first time Nathan visited David, it was to rebuke him for his adultery. This time, Nathan comes to congratulate David and gives the following word: "And He (God) sent word by the hand of Nathan the prophet: so he called his name Jedidiah, because of the LORD" (2 Samuel 12:25).

Nathan's good words of comfort prompted David again to give another name to Solomon, *Jedidiah* meaning *"beloved of Yah (Yahweh)."* Thus, the new son was a sign to David, he had truly been forgiven. When God forgives, He forgets the old sin forever see Psalm 103:12.

So if you have made a mistake, it doesn't mean God is done with you. Quite the contrary. Every mistake you make and truly repent stirs a new move of God in your life. This blessing only manifests when you are able to let go of your disappointments and move forward knowing God is with you.

STARTING OVER

Many people think that their past is all that they have. They ruminate on the past, because it's easier to see than an uncertain future. At some point in their life, many people feel like David. Perhaps, they committed a terrible sin and that sin made them feel guilty, ashamed, and condemned. Perhaps they have asked God for mercy and forgiveness, but somehow their heart still condemns them, like a knife cutting deep. As a result of their guilt and shame, they lack the confidence to move forward in life.

Thankfully, how we sometimes feel can be far from the truth. Realigning our minds with the truth of God's word will free us from the lies and guilt of the enemy. The scripture says God's mercies are new every day (see Lamentation 3:22-23). Also, if you recall the event of David above with his sin with Bathsheba, you will see how God forgave him completely when he repented. God always responds positively to a sincere repentant heart. David knew intimately the forgiveness of God that is available to not only him but everyone who calls on the Lord. Hear David's declarations of God's faithfulness in his psalm, "He (God) will not always strive with us, nor will He keep His anger forever."(Psalm 103:9).

From David's lesson, we know with confidence no matter what wrong anyone did yesterday, if repented, God is no longer angry. If feelings of guilt or condemnation arise, we can rest in the scripture that states, "If we confess our sins, he is faithful and just to forgive us our sins, and to cleanse us from all unrighteousness." Any condemnation after this fact is an attack by Satan. The way to overcome this attack is to realize God's love and favor over your life right now. Begin by thanking God for His forgiveness and favor over your life.

THE HIDDEN BLESSINGS

Many people are very positive "every disappointment is a blessing," even though only a few have made the decision to let go of disappointments. The hidden blessings we can all get from disappointments are the lessons we learn while being in the trial. This is because learning from our disappointments will *equip* and *empower* us to avoid making similar mistakes in the future.

Additionally, the lessons we learn and heed from our own disappointments can be a *lifesaver* for someone else who may be walking into a similar situation. Think about David and the lesson he learned from his Bathsheba's experience. His final words to his successor, Solomon, encouraged him to hold onto the lesson David cherished as his strength: "As for you, my son Solomon, know the God of your father, and serve Him with a loyal heart and with a willing mind; for the Lord searches all hearts and understands all the intent of the thoughts. If you seek Him, He will be found of you; but if you forsake Him, He will cast you off forever" (1 Chronicles 28:9).

In other words, we cannot hide anything from God. If we sinned against Him, we won't go unpunished. Unfortunately, Solomon was quick to forget David's important lesson and lost ten tribes of his kingdom to his servant. The two God spared were because of God's faithfulness to the promise He gave David not because of Solomon (see 1 Chronicles 17:13-14 and 1 Kings 11:9-13). I encourage you to learn and heed the lessons of your past failures and be willing to learn from the mistakes others have made. Ultimately, if you want to bury your disappointments and start new again, you must learn to discern the opportunities the Lord has for you in your present season and take advantage of them.

CHAPTER 9

DISCERNING THE SEASONS

*"Of the sons of Issachar who had understanding of
the times, to know what Israel ought to do..."*
2 Chronicles 12: 32

Season is a definite period of time fixed by God for a particular purpose to happen. This means every season has a purpose, and every purpose has a season. Things don't just happen. They have a right time to happen. The wise King Solomon states it this way: "To everything there is a season, A time for every purpose under heaven" (Ecclesiastes 3:1). If we study the words of Solomon deeper, we notice God has put everything in our lives, the big and small, good and bad into seasons.

"A time to be born, and a time to die; a time to plant, and a time to pluck what is planted; A time to kill, and a time to heal; a time to break down, and a time to build up; A time to weep, and a time to laugh; a time to mourn, and a time to dance; A time to cast away stones, and a time to gather stones" (Ecclesiastes 3:2–13).

There is a season to get married, start your education, ministry or business, begin a job, buy a house, or book an appointment. The list is endless. It also means there are certain things that won't happen in your life unless you're in the season. The implication of this truth is if you fail to discern the season, you may end up forfeiting the opportunity or blessing it carries. Worse, when we fail to discern the season, we feel needlessly frustrated wanting a different season instead of embracing the season we are in. It may take you years to recover from being out of sync with the season you are experiencing when you fall into one of those traps. Sadly no one can skip a season to go forward faster, or rewind a season to relive it again.

As much as we may want out of a season of hardship or suffering and into another of blessing, every season in God's timetable is equally important. Every season holds blessings and opportunities, even in periods of attacks, delay, or discouragement. You may be wondering what blessings or opportunities can be in a season of delay, disappointment or failure. The first one that comes immediately to mind is the opportunity to grow and mature spiritually. In fact, seasons of delay, disappointment and failure are the best times to grow and mature in faith (see James 1: 2-3, 1 Peter 5:10). Secondly, these seasons prepare us for the next season of harvest or plenty. In other words, where you are now will qualify you for where you desire to be. The season you are in right now is exactly where you need to be. It is preparing you for tomorrow. Delay is preparing you for acceleration, disappointment for divine appointments, and failure for victory tomorrow.

Every season has purpose. Until you fulfill that purpose, you are not qualified for the next season. In much the same way a student cannot be promoted to the next grade if they fail their exams, we often repeat difficult seasons until we learn the lessons. God's plan is for us to fulfill His ultimate goal for our lives in phases. If you are in an uncomfortable season currently, I have encouraging news: ***this season will change.*** Daniel, a man of God in the Old Testament, affirms this truth: "And He (God) changes times and the seasons; He removes kings and raises up kings" (Daniel 2:21).

Things will not always be the way they are right now. Your situation will not always be bleak or difficult. Things are going to change for good. Trust God for your change of season in the perfect time. However, the fact that the current season will change may not be good news for some. Those who don't like change, won't enjoy this news. Neither will those who are enjoying their present season. Where you are is still not where you should be in the future. There's a better place for you. Don't be afraid of your next season; it will lead you to greater things.

If you resist change, you won't be able to fulfill God's ultimate purpose for your life. God designed these changes to happen in our lives. In the Book of Daniel, it said, "He (God) changes the times and the seasons." Therefore, it's not you or me bringing change into our lives, it is God. He changes our seasons in order to fulfill His purposes in us. God is the true world changer and the designer of change. You're responsible to discern the current season and work within it accordingly.

Discernment: A Gift

Discernment, according to 1828 *Webster Dictionary*, is "the act of discerning, also the power of faculty of the mind, by which it distinguishes one thing from another as truth from falsehood, virtue from vice, acuteness of judgment, power of perceiving differences of things or ideas, and their relations and tendencies." The key word from this definition is "distinguish." The term distinguish is to recognize and understand the difference between two or more things or ideas. Putting this concept into context, we need to understand our current season and work within it. To discern means to distinguish or to differentiate one season from another, God's purpose from yours and God's voice from Satan's and even yours.

Every Believer needs discernment to understand the seasons. Prioritizing or seeking discernment when confused about the seasons is something every Christian needs to do, especially as we are in the final days. Jesus warned the end days would be associated with massive deception: false Christ, false prophets, false teachers and false doctrines. However, the Bible shows us two ways a Christian can gain discernment. One comes as a gift from the Holy Spirit. "There are diversities of gifts, but the same Spirit...For to one is given the word of wisdom through the Spirit...to another discerning of spirits" (1Corinthians12:4-10).

Some Believers are gifted in the church by the Holy Spirit to distinguish between the spirits behind action: God, demonic, and human. This gift also enables Believers to differentiate between those who speak the truth from those who are under the influence of the lying spirit. If you don't have this gift, you can earnestly seek it in prayer (2 Corinthians 12:31). Even as a gift, it still needs to be honed continually through the study of God's Word.

The second way of gaining discernment is through your everyday experience with God and His Word. "But solid food belongs to those who are of full age, that is, those who by reason of use have their senses exercised to discern both good and evil" (Hebrew 5: 14). This scripture means as you grow and mature in your personal relationship with the Lord through study of God's Word, the Holy Spirit uses it to train your senses (hearing, sight, feelings) to be able to distinguish between what is from God and what is not. This is another reason why spiritual growth should be a priority to every Christian.

So how can you discern your season? The answer is simple: discern God's purpose, that is, the thoughts and the intents in God's Heart for you. When you discern God's purpose for you and what area you need growth, you've discerned your season. This discernment comes to us through the Holy Spirit in the form of a word, a word in season.

A Word In Season

God desires earnestly to communicate His purpose to each of His children so they can take advantage of it to advance their lives and His kingdom here on earth. The way He does this is through His Spirit conveying and revealing His thoughts and intentions for us in the form of a word, either spoken audibly from Him or through one of His faithful servants, sent to us in a vision or dream, or quietly impressed in our hearts (an inward prompting). Whatever way God chooses to reveal His purposes to us, our responsibility is to discern, believe, and heed the instruction it holds.

Being able to discern or recognize what God's purpose and plans are is one of the reasons God gave His Spirit. The Holy Spirit draws from the Father and Jesus and downloads that desire into our spirits. This is why in Paul's first letter to the Corinthians he wrote: "But as it is written: Eye has not seen, nor ear heard, nor have entered into the heart of man, the things which God has prepared for those who love Him. But God has revealed them unto us through His Spirit: for the Spirit searches all things, yes, the deep things of God. For what man knows the things of man except the spirit of the man which is in him? Even so no one knows the things of God except the Spirit of God. Now we have received, not the spirit of the world, but the Spirit who is from God, that we might know the things that have been freely given to us by God" (1 Corinthians 2:9-12).

The key words you should notice are *"Now we have received, not the spirit of the world, but the Spirit who is from God, that we might know the things that have been freely given us by God."* In other words, God desires us to know what's in His heart for us. The Holy Spirit is the one who is carrying out this job. That was exactly why Jesus said it was for our advantage He went away, so that our Helper (the Holy Spirit) would come, because there are still many things Jesus wants to tell us. Being without the Holy Spirit, we cannot discern or understand them (see John 16:5-15). In fact, without the Holy Spirit, Believers can't know

God's plan because the Holy Spirit is the one who accesses God's heart and shows it to us.

As Believers, this is good news. It's also bad news for the enemy, because it keeps the enemy completely ignorant concerning God's plans and purpose for the Believer. In other words, God's purpose for Believers is like a classified government document to the enemy. He only knows what you leak to him. Be careful what you give away. This is what Paul's emphasis in verse 7, 8 in the above passage. Sadly, this is not good news for the person without Christ too, for as Paul continues: "But the natural man does not receive the things of the Spirit of God, for they are foolishness to him; nor can he know them, because they are spiritually discerned" (1 Corinthians 2:14).

This means the natural man, a person without Christ, a person who is not saved, even if he or she has been in church for years, cannot know God's purpose, God's will or desires for their lives. Revelation comes from the Holy Spirit, which the world cannot receive (John 14:17).

Additionally, a babe in Christ or a spiritually immature Believer is often not able to discern God's purpose for their life due to the lack of relationship or knowledge of God. If by the reason of a spiritual gifting, the spiritually immature believer is able to discern, their discernment will be with limitations. Only mature believers can truly discern the activities of the Holy Spirit. See these scriptures below: "But solid food is for full-grown men, for those whose senses and mental faculties are trained by practice to discriminate and distinguish between what is morally good and noble and what is evil and contrary either to divine or human" (Hebrew 5:14 AMP). In Romans 8:14, it says, "The mature children of God are those who are moved by the impulses of the Holy Spirit" (TPT).

Notice both scriptures confirm only mature children of God are able to discern what is of God and what is not. This is why new Believers in Christ need to grow up.

Growing Up

Believers who are still relatively spiritually immature cannot discern or understand what God's Spirit is saying or prompting them to do, because they are dull or slow to hearing spiritual things. This is why the writer of Hebrews wrote: "Of whom we have much to say, and hard to explain, since you have become dull of hearing" (Hebrews 5:11).

Notice the writer said there were things he wanted to say to these Believers, but they were too hard to explain to some of them because of their inability to understand. But why are some Believers slow in understanding? Simply, their flesh is their stumbling blocking. In fact, the flesh is the only thing blocking Believers from receiving all that Jesus bought and paid for us to have. This is why we are called to die to ourselves, that is, to put away the flesh's ruling over our lives. The apostle Paul puts it this way: "When I was a child, I spoke as a child, I understood as a child, I thought as a child; but when I became a man, I put away childish things" (1Corinthians 13:11).

To become spiritually mature, we must put off childish things. Childish things in this scripture denote selfish things: things we want but not what God wants. They may be things our flesh craves but not what the Spirit desires. I have two toddlers at home and also manage many others in our school. I can tell you by their very nature, kids want everything centered around them. Several times, Lily will take our daughter along with her to the market to buy food. As a caring mom, she will use the opportunity to buy any snacks for Sherrill that she can afford. Often they aren't the brand Sherrill likes, and she will refuse them and start crying. Oftentimes, she will cry till they get home. As a result, Lily stopped taking her along when she went to the market to avoid being embarrassed. The problem is Sherrill doesn't understand her mother or her mother's reasons. Instead, she wants her mother to understand her because she is self-seeking. This is how children behave in most situations. They always desire their own way and not the other way around. Thankfully, as they grow, they begin to put away their self-interest and seek for the good of the family and others.

Similarly, this is also true for Believers. We all begin spiritually immature, seeking our own interest. This is part of the reason we don't hear or understand God's voice or inner promptings. Thankfully, as we grow in Christ and learn to put aside our selfish desires, we begin to seek the desires of God's heart. As we seek Him and His kingdom, we begin to hear His voice more clearly with more understanding, which helps us mature faster.

This is why Paul calls Believers to put away childish things: our selfish and lustful desires and cravings. Paul knew the more we put away the flesh, the more we grow. The more we grow, the more we are able to discern what God's Spirit is saying or prompting in each season. The more we discern and lean into God's leading, the more we become like Christ.

So how do we put away the flesh which is our stumbling block? How do we help our new nature grow? The answer to both these questions is continuous study and application of God's Word. God's Word is the spiritual nourishment our new nature requires to mature and bring forth good fruit (see John 8:31, Colossians 3: 15, 2 Timothy 3:15-17, Hebrews 5:12, James 1:21-25, 1Peter 2:2). However, no matter how spiritually mature you are right now, every Believer still needs more growth, because the goal of full spiritual maturity is to become like Jesus Christ. Until you are walking continually in love and obedience to the Holy Spirit, walking on water, raising the dead, and performing the countless miracles of Jesus for his glory, you still have room to grow and mature.

Let's look at two Biblical stories that illustrate how spiritual maturity can position Believers to discern and break into unexpected great seasons of life.

NEHEMIAH DISCERNS THE SEASON

Let's look at the life of Nehemiah for a moment. Ask yourself, "What do I know about him?" Here is a brief profile of him: Nehemiah was a young Jewish man who served as King Artaxerxes' cupbearer in the Persian Empire. One day, one of his kinsmen came to him from Judah. Nehemiah asked him about the welfare of the Jews who had survived Babylonian captivity and of Jerusalem in general. The report he received was bad news. He was told his people were in great reproach, and Jerusalem was lying in ruins. This news broke Nehemiah's heart and brought him to his knees weeping and repenting before God in prayer. He fasted on the behalf of his people and nation. It was at this moment, God put a plan in Nehemiah's heart to go and build the walls of Jerusalem and to strengthen His people spiritually who lived there. As soon as Nehemiah received this word in season from God for a new direction, he sought permission from his boss the king to leave his post temporarily to return to Jerusalem and do what God put in his heart. While his request would have normally been an offense before the king, God gave him favor with the king. In fact, God gave him favor with everyone needed to assist him with the building of the walls and provided materials for building.

Without any delay, Nehemiah left for Jerusalem to begin his new job. Eventually, through God's continuous help, Nehemiah and his team were able to complete the building of Jerusalem's wall despite the oppositions against them. Once the wall was achieved, he led a spiritual reformation to bring God's people back to seek and worship their one true God. With the help of Ezra the scribe, Nehemiah's selfless services won him a promotion to become governor of Jerusalem. At the end, his story went from being a cupbearer to the king to a spiritual leader and eventually a governor.

Nehemiah's life is a wonderful example of a spiritually mature Believer, as mature believers don't seek their own. He didn't seek his own good, but the good of his people and His God. The vision for his people's restoration led him to seek God for a way to help them and found greater favor with God. Here is the point I want you to understand: Nehemiah's spiritual maturity helped him to be sensitive to what was in God's heart for him at that season. He knew what God's plan for him was and the risk involved, yet he did not hesitate to step down from a prestigious and royal job with all the security and luxury it offered. Instead, without any delay, Nehemiah stepped out into an uncertain future. His faithfulness secured his name on the good side of Biblical history.

The life lesson for Believers to learn from Nehemiah is this: God can change your season suddenly. He has the ability to change what you're doing presently without any prior notice. This sudden change of season will happen to all of us. The goal is for God to promote or advance our lives forward. When seasons change, it takes those who are spiritually sensitive (a characteristic of spiritual mature believers) to be able to discern and respond to it in confidence and without delay. That was my story when I stepped into ministry from my secular job. Even though I was already preparing for ministry like I shared in an earlier chapter, the season came at an unexpected time. Like Nehemiah, I was sensitive to discern it. Without delay I notified my boss and left to begin the strategic planning to launch into full-time ministry. When Believers step out in God's season, they enjoy His favor, provision, protection and general support.

On the other hand, spiritually immature Believers will be so concerned with only their own welfare, they won't be able to discern the direction God is moving. The thought or fear of risking their current good life by quitting a prestigious job offering them security and luxury prevents them from stepping into an even better future. Instead, immature Believers attempt to delay things until they feel conditions are favorable. Unfortunately, this is the kind of attitude that keeps many Believers bound to one spot longer than they should stay. If this is your case, you can break free through submission to God's word. Now let's consider the second story from the New Testament that will challenge you to spiritual maturity.

Paul's Second Missionary Journey

In Acts Chapter 16:4-10, something happened that changed history. Bible scholars believed that this moment also affected civilization today, impacting you and me directly. It's the story of how God used the apostle Paul in his second missionary journey to carry the gospel of Jesus Christ to Europe instead of further into Asia as Paul had planned.

Paul had embarked on this planned missionary trip with his team to return to the churches he and Barnabas had established on his first journey. The goal was to deliver to the churches the decree of the Jerusalem Council, as well strengthen the churches in that region and plant new ones. As they travelled through Asia, their work appeared to be gaining progress in that region (Acts 16:5) until the Holy Spirit showed up with a new plan. Firstly, He forbade Paul from preaching any further in Asia. So Paul and his team moved on to Mysia and Bithynia, but the Holy Spirit would not permit him to minister there either.

You might pause to consider why would God do that? Isn't preaching the gospel to the lost, the heartbeat of God? Why would God delay saving souls when there was a preacher willing to go? I'll answer these questions shortly.

Then, Paul and his team continued their journey until they arrived at Troas, where Paul had a vision in the night of a man beckoning on him to come to Macedonia to help them. At that moment, Paul knew for sure the Lord was calling them to preach the gospel in Macedonia. He began to head West towards Europe instead of East towards Asia. Paul's entire plans and itinerary changed by obeying the Holy Spirit. Remember, Macedonia wasn't Paul's initial target audience, but he obeyed it with prompt obedience. This kind of prompt obedience can only result from a firm conviction, a character often associated with mature Believers. The King James Version puts it this way: "And after he had seen the vision, immediately we endeavored to go into Macedonia, assuredly gathering that the Lord had called us to preach the gospel unto them" (Acts 16:10).

Notice the word, "assuredly." It means "definitely or certainly." This means Paul was absolutely certain without any doubt this was what God wanted him to do. Paul knew also that his initial plans meant nothing compared to God's leading. Paul was as certain of this new direction for the gospel as he was in previous times when the Holy Spirit forbade him from preaching in Asia.

Now back to our questions. Why did God want Paul to go West to Europe instead of East to Asia? Here is what many Bible scholars share: it is because God in His perfect and awesome wisdom knew that at that moment in history, the Gospel of Jesus Christ would grow more exponentially in Europe than in Asia. By the gospel spreading to Europe at that time, it eventually reached the entire world. In other words, Europe was good ground for the seed of the Gospel of Jesus Christ.

Now let me ask you, what do you think would be the response of a spiritually immature Believer to the kind of vision Paul received? Chances are he or she would first seek interpretations or confirmations before acting. Of course, confirmation has its place in Christian living, but that is not the type of confirmation I am speaking about. Essentially, an immature Believer is typically surrounded with a social-spiritual circle of doubters and naysayers, discouraging obedience. It is also likely, the immature Believer would want signs like the Pharisees in Jesus' days, to be absolutely certain before they obeyed. In the end, the answers from the doubters and naysayers would overwhelm his or her heart to the point he/she would be so discouraged, he/she would resolve to continue with the status quo. Sadly, this Believer would lose the opportunity of serving God in a far greater capacity. Thankfully, Paul was a mature Believer who was able to discern God's voice and the leading of the Holy Spirit to advance God's kingdom in an exponential way.

No matter where you're at spiritually, I challenge you to continue to pursue spiritual maturity. Spiritual maturity is the purpose of every delay, disappointment or failure you face. Take advantage of your delay, disappointments and failure seasons to grow spiritually, because those who fail to grow will end up losing the blessings and opportunities of their seasons.

Man-Made Delays & Failures

Sometimes, we create our own delays, disappointments and failures, if we are not careful to discern our seasons or how we ought to respond to them. One practical example is the children of Abraham (the Israelites) who were supposed to stay in Egypt for only four hundred years (see Genesis 15:13) but end up staying four hundred and thirty years (Exodus 12:41). That was an extra thirty years of affliction, suffering, and bondage simply because they failed to discern their season when God raised Moses as their deliverer. Let's look to see how they failed to discern their season of their deliverance: "Finally, the time came for God to do what he had promised Abraham. By then the number of our people in Egypt had greatly increased. Another king was ruling Egypt, and he didn't know anything about Joseph" (Acts 7:17-18 CEV). The scriptures says again in Acts, chapter 7, verses 23-24, "When Moses was forty years old, he wanted to help the Israelites because they were his own people. One day he saw an Egyptian mistreating one of them. So he rescued the man and killed the Egyptian".

Notice the first scripture above says, *"finally, the time came for God to do what he had promised Abraham."* In other words, it was time for God to initiate Israel's freedom process. At this time, Israel was at three-hundred-ninety years in bondage, just ten years away from God's promised freedom to Abraham. God's plan was to use Moses to obtain their freedom in the next ten years. Moses was aware of God's desire for him to be used as the catalyst for the nation's freedom: "Moses thought the rest of his people would realize that God was going to use him to set them free. But they didn't understand" (Acts 7:25 CEV).

In other words, Stephen said God was already moving in Moses' heart, but Israel, his people, failed to discern the timing because they weren't spiritually sensitive or mature. Since they were spiritually dense, they didn't know it was time for their deliverance. Since they were dull of hearing, God used their discouraging circumstance to signal them: "Now it happened in the process of time that the king of Egypt died. Then the children of Israel groaned because of the bondage, and they cried out; and their cry came up to God because of the bondage" (Exodus 2: 23).

In other words, their hardship caused them to pray, and their prayers touched God's heart. I believe Israel would have spent more years in Egypt if their suffering wasn't intentionally increased. Comfortability often keeps Believers to stay where they should not. Affliction and trials motivate us to seek change. The sad fact is many of God's people are presently spending more years in their own Egypt, beyond God's original timeline, because they are too comfortable with their circumstances. Yet, a time of mercy will come to create an increase in the situational intensity, where Believers finally seek a way out. Such was the way for the Jews. Now after the Israelites had rejected Moses, he fled to the wilderness. When Moses was in the wilderness, Israel's affliction intensified, and they finally prayed. Hear what God told Moses at the burning bush: "And the Lord said: 'I have surely seen the oppression of My people who are in Egypt, and have heard their cry because of their taskmasters, for I know their sorrows. So I have come down to deliver them out of the hand of the Egyptians'" (Exodus 3:7-8).

Did you catch that? God was committed to the promise He gave to Abraham their father, but He still did nothing until they invited Him into the situation. They waited an extra thirty years of suffering before they finally cried out to God who then told Moses. The example from Israel is true for how God works in the lives of Believers today. Even though God has given us a promise, He still wants us to remind and invite Him into our situation. Why? Because God has given us free will and won't infringe upon it. Now, learn the difference from Israel between the spiritually mature and immature follower of God. Immature Believers wait until their situation is more than they can handle before calling out to God. Sadly, they often experience additional misery as a result. Spiritually mature Believers discern God's purpose and move with it. They don't need for the situation to become so uncomfortable or out of control before they seek God. Mature believers are walking in daily communion with God, and you can too.

Maximizing The Seasons

Being spiritually mature doesn't just help us to discern the seasons, it also helps maximize the season's opportunities. Perhaps you wonder, what that means? Let's look to the apostle Paul who wrote to encourage the Ephesian church, "Redeeming the time, because the days are evil." (Ephesians 5:16 NKJV). The NIV put it this way, "Make the most of every opportunity." Paul is saying Christians need to utilize the season by getting the best out of it while they can, because a time may be coming when they cannot. Therefore, to maximize our seasons means to get as much advantage or good opportunities that we can from our present situation.

The world will not give Christians what belongs to us in Christ. We have to demand it. That is why Jesus said in Matthew 11:12:"And from the days of John the Baptist until now the kingdom of heaven suffers violence, and the violent take it by force." In our context, "to be violent" means to be quick to recognize an opportunity, especially one based on the promise of God, and take advantage of it immediately. This was exactly what Jephthah, the Gileadite, exemplified. Initially, his kinsmen thrust him out of his father's house because his mother was a harlot. Yet, when the Ammonites started war, the Israelites looked to Jephthah to lead them into battle. Look at the reply Jephthah gave them: "So Jephthah said to the elders of Gilead, 'If you take me back home to fight against the people of Ammon, and the Lord delivers them to me, shall I be your head?'" (Judges 11:9)

While one would think war was a terrible trial, Jephthah recognized an opportunity not only to help his people, but to earn back his rightful position in his father's house. He took advantage of this opportunity, won the war, and became ruler over those who had previously mistreated him. Jephthah could have walked away, angry from his past, and let Israel be defeated in the war. However, if he had done that, he too would have suffered great harm from the Ammonites, possibly even death.

God wants us to grow spiritually so we can recognize and make the most of every opportunity. Even opportunities that seem negative can be used for our good. God gives each of us the opportunity we need to succeed in life. However, each Believer must recognize these opportunities in the right season to make the most of them. If we fail to work within our season properly, we miss out on the blessings and growth.

CHAPTER 10

Why Pray?

"Make haste, O God, to deliver me!
Make haste to help me, O Lord!"
Psalm 70:1

Never underestimate the power of prayer. It's one virtue changing countless lives all over the world. This is why prayer should be very important to you, especially in your seasons of delays, disappointments and failures. Our prayers are important to God. Here are three reasons our prayers are important to God, especially in our troubling seasons:

Prayer Creates and Maintains an Intimate Relationship With God

Our prayers help to build a bond between God and us, the same way positive communication builds bonds between parents and their children, a husband and wife, or best friends. Communication is a two-way street. Both parties listen as well as speak. As our ability to listen and speak freely grows, so does our trust and understanding of the other person. Sadly many Christians wouldn't make time to talk to the Lord if they didn't face opposition or trials. This is why sometimes the Lord allows difficult circumstances in our lives. He wants to give us the opportunity to build a close intimate relationship with Him. Prayer enables us to triumph over our circumstances and opposition. David, Daniel, Jesus, and the apostles all maintained a wonderful relationship with the Father through their daily prayers, even in moments of trials and tribulations (Daniel 6:10, Acts 1:14, 3:1, Matthew 14:23, Psalms 55:17). They are all men of extraordinary victories too. God doesn't just want us to overcome the current attack; He desires us to be in continual victory. This is what a lifestyle of prayer makes happen.

PRAYER IS A SIGN OF OUR DEPENDENCY AND RELIABILITY ON GOD

Believers need to be completely dependent upon God for an abundant life. Jesus stated in John 15:4-5, "Abide in me, and I in you. As the branch cannot bear fruit of itself, except it abides in the vine; no more can ye, except ye abide in me. I am the vine, ye are the branches: He that abides in me, and I in him, the same bringeth forth much fruit: for without me ye can do nothing." Without God, we can do nothing. God knows He is essential for us to live and be victorious to bear good fruit. He wants us to come to Him for help. Depending on God is a sign of trust on our part and honors Him greatly. In fact, God was so keenly aware of our need for Him above all things, that He expressly forbade His people from seeking anything above Him (Exodus 20:3, Deuteronomy 5:7).

PRAYER IS AN INVITATION TO GOD TO INTERVENE IN OUR CIRCUMSTANCE

When we pray, we are submitting our will to God and asking Him to come and take over our battle. Myles Munroe called prayer, "a license." That is, prayer is giving God the license to intervene on earth (see Psalm 115:16). God is sovereign and rules heaven and the earth. Yet, He put mankind in charge of the earth through Adam. While Adam lost that authority to Satan, Jesus got it back. While most of the world is under the current rule of Satan, Believers have the blessed opportunity to ask Jesus, the real owner of the earth, to intervene on their behalf and overcome the enemy. God doesn't typically interfere in our affairs unless we give Him permission.

Remember the Israelites in Egypt we discussed in the previous chapter? Even though God committed a promise to Abraham regarding his descendants' freedom, until they cried out to God in their hardship, He did nothing to intervene. The moment they earnestly prayed, God came down to deliver them. Their prayers gave Him the right to step into their situation. It has been said that, "God will do nothing except you pray." Don't face your trials alone. Invite God into them. He wants to help you.

We see from Old Testament scriptures that as powerful as prayers can be, sometimes they are resisted or hindered by the devil and his demons (see Daniel 10:12-13). This is why Believers need to pray an irresistible prayer. But what is irresistible prayer? On one side, irresistible prayer is a prayer that the enemy cannot withstand or stymie, at least not for long. While on the other side, irresistible prayer is a prayer that is so attractive to God, it's sure to receive an answer. Irresistible prayer is a save my soul (SMS) O Lord prayer. It's for an emergency rescue, the same way an SOS (save our souls) message is sent for emergency rescue. This is exactly what David did in a time of his life when he faced distress: "But I am poor and needy; make haste to me, O God! You are my help and my deliverer; O Lord, do not delay" (Psalm 70:5).

Notice David says, *"make haste O God...do not delay."* In other words, David is saying, "save my soul, O God, because if you delay then I'm finished." This should be our attitude in our season of delay, disappointment and failure. Pray like you don't have any more time.

CHAPTER 11

7 Irresistible Prayers

"But when ye pray, use not vain repetitions, as the unbelievers do: for they think that they shall be heard for their much speaking."
Matthew 6:7

Let me show you seven ways you can pray irresistibly so God can come to your rescue before things go too far. Note: these are not listed in any particular order. Most Believers need to combine or all several of these prayer styles for ultimate results. Always use the ones you need at the moment depending on how the Holy Spirit leads you in prayer.

Stand in Righteousness When You Pray

The earnest prayer of a righteous person has great power and wonderful results. (James 5:16 NLT)

God's Word above says the earnest or heartfelt prayer of a *righteous* person, not a *sinner*, provides great power and wonderful results. In other words, when a righteous person prays, there will be so much power flow from God to open closed doors, heal the sick, and provide all kinds of breakthroughs or other amazing miracles. The scripture says, "The righteous are bold as a lion" (Proverbs 28:1). In other words, living righteously empowers Believers to come to God's throne of grace with boldness and confidence. This is the kind of attitude that secures help from God's throne. Simply put, righteousness opens the door to God's power and sin closes that door. (See Isaiah 59:1-2, Psalm 66:18). Thankfully, as Believers in Christ, you have been made right with God in your relationship through Christ. *Jesus has made you righteous.* Believers have the right through Christ to pray with great power and have wonderful results. Therefore, start praying now in faith and see what God's power will do.

However, if you are a double-minded believer, compromising a little here and a little there, then this benefit of prayer James is talking about is not for you. While Jesus has made you righteous before God, you cannot live a life of active sin and expect God to not deal with your sin on earth. For scripture says a man must be a worshipper of God and do God's will before God will hear him (John 9:31). God is under no obligation to listen to the prayers of sinners, with the exception of their prayer for repentance. Many of our delays, disappointments and failures result from our active sin. We need to release these sinful habits before the situations created by them will end. Nevertheless, if you find yourself giving into sin, you can still come boldly to God's throne of grace to receive mercy and forgiveness, because God wants to clean you from your sinful lifestyle. When we confess our sins, God is merciful and just to forgive us (1 John 1:9). Standing before God cleansed again, we can pray boldly for help. After repenting from any sinful lifestyle, see how quickly God will rescue you. However, if you decide to harden your heart against sin, the scripture warns us, "Be sure your sin will find you out" (Number 32:23).

There is another group of people for whom the advice of James will not work, and that is unsaved men and women. Those who have never received the forgiveness of God He offered to all mankind through the sacrificial death of His beloved Son, Jesus Christ, on the cross cannot pray the prayer of a righteous man. However, they can call upon the name of the Lord through Jesus and be saved. Upon salvation, God immediately recognizes a new Believer as righteous. This gives them instantaneous access to praying a righteous prayer.

PRAY WITH EXPECTATION AND FAITH

"Therefore I say unto you, what things soever you desire, when you pray, believe that you receive them, and you shall have them." (Mark 11:24)

Without confident expectation and faith, you won't get much from God. Notice Jesus says, *"when you pray."* That means you must believe as you are praying, not at some later time when you have confirmation or a sign. Your faith must be alive, believing God has heard you and will answer, in the moment of your prayer. Therefore, pray until you know for sure you've received what you asked from Him. Though it may not be visible at this time, your conviction is firm.

In the fight of faith, firm conviction, not doubt, is what empowers you to receive from God. Take a look at the words of James: "But let him ask in faith, with no doubting, for he who doubts is like a wave of the sea driven and tossed by the wind, for let not that man suppose that he will receive anything from the Lord" (James 1: 6-7).

Did you get that? Doubt or unbelief hinders Believers from receiving from God. The Bible reveals the only thing that hindered the flow of God's power from working through Jesus at one point in His ministry was the unbelief of His hometown people: "Now he could do no mighty work there, except that He laid His hands on a few sick people and healed them. and He marveled because of their unbelief" (Mark 6:5-6). I love how Brother Lawrence, the French Monk, commented on faith: "The trust we put in God honors Him much, and draws down great graces." His words are drawn from the scripture: "But without faith no one can please God. We must believe that God is real and that He rewards everyone who searches for Him" (Hebrews 11:6 CEV).

I encourage you to pray with confidence that God hears you and that you've received your petitions asked of Him. Expect the manifestation with perseverance.

BE SPECIFIC WHEN YOU PRAY

"What do you want me to do for you?" Luke 18:41

In Jesus' ministry on earth, when people came to him for help, these words were Jesus' favorite response, "What do you want Me to do for you?" Essentially, Jesus was asking for the person to be specific about what he or she wanted from him. Blind Bartimaeus was one of those people who received what he requested. His was a one-line prayer: "Rabboni, that I may receive my sight" (Mark 10:51). Bartimaeus didn't tell Jesus a long story. He got straight to the point. The answer to his request was immediate! He received his sight. Even now, Jesus is asking Believers, "What do you want Me to do for You?"

Another biblical example of praying specific prayer is Hannah. Hannah went to the annual Shiloh worship event with her husband, but this particular year the Bible recorded her demands of the LORD. In tears she asked a specific request: 'Give Your maidservant a MALE child.'

Notice, she didn't ask for God to give her any child, but specifically a male child: "Then she [Hannah] made a vow and said, "O Lord of hosts, if you will indeed look on the affliction of Your maidservant and remember me, and not forget Your maidservant, but will give Your maidservant a male child, then I will give him to the Lord all the days of his life, and no razor shall come upon his head" (1 Samuel 1:11).

Hannah was specific and clear about what she wanted from God. This is what I call **planned prayer**. A planned prayer is a prayer that details what you want exactly and why you want it. This kind of prayer takes faith because it can specifically acknowledge whether or not the prayer was answered when the answer manifests. Solomon, when he became king of Israel, also prayed this kind of prayer. There was no beating around the bush (See 1 Kings 3:5 -13) or being ambiguous.

God isn't interested in a "shotgun prayer," the kind of prayer that doesn't really have a specific target or know what is being requested. Essentially, a shotgun prayer occurs when Believer generalizes a request and has no solid way of knowing whether or not the prayer was answered in the future. These prayers often are disguised as being submissive to God's will, but in reality, they lack true faith for the clarity of what is being requested. Shotgun prayers often include a lot of "buts" to cover doubts about God's ability to fulfill the request or are based in a lack of understanding God's will in the situation. Believers who don't know the will of God in an area often pray a shotgun prayer hoping to cover all the bases. It's like a scattered prayer, hoping just one point might gain God's attention. Often Believers mistake a shotgun prayer as being similar to Jesus in the Garden, "not my will but yours be done." Sadly, this is not the case. Jesus knew God's will in his situation required his death. His prayer for another way out was based on his flesh's desire to not suffer, but ultimately his plea, "not my will but yours be done" was a submission of his flesh to the Father's known will. Jesus never prayed from a position of not knowing God's purpose in his life or the situation. Jesus never prayed a shotgun prayer. The Gospels are full of Jesus' specific prayer requests, as evidenced in their specific fulfillment on earth in miracles.

Praying specific prayers allows a Believer to give thanks and gratitude when the prayer is answered. If there is no specific request, there can be no specific fulfillment. Thus, a Believer cannot grow in faith or confidence in his or her prayer life. Having the ability to reflect back on answered prayer provides a solid record of events from which one can gain strength and encouragement.

PRAY ACCORDING TO GOD'S WILL

"And this is the confidence that we have in him [God], that, if we ask anything according to his [God's] will, he heareth us, And if we know that he hears us, whatsoever we ask, we know that we have the petitions that we desire of him." 1 John 5:14-15 (KJV)

God's will is not a mystery. He has clearly expressed His will through his son, Jesus Christ, and throughout the Scriptures. Ephesians chapter 1 tells us God has made His will known in Jesus, which is affirmed in 1 Corinthians 2:7-8. Through our connection to Christ via the indwelling presence of the Holy Spirit, we have access to know the will of God. Setting aside our desired outcomes and emotions is often more difficult than knowing God's will in most situations. In the areas where we don't know the will of God, we can earnestly seek it in prayer. Knowing when we ask for wisdom, God will give it to us (James 1:5-8). We can also pray in the Spirit, who being One with the Father knows the will of God and intercedes for us (Romans 8:26-27). Unfortunately, allowing ourselves to pray in the Spirit is something many Christians feel is uncomfortable because it involves praying in another language they may not understand. While praying in other tongues as led by the Spirit may be unpopular in many Christian communities being misunderstood, it is firmly rooted in the Bible. The Apostle Paul encouraged Believers to seek the gifts of the Spirit and wished they could all speak in tongues (1 Corinthians 14:5). God's truths remain true and are for our best, whether we embrace them or not. Like Paul, I hope you seek God for this gift of the Spirit so you can enjoy the fullness of God's power working through the Holy Spirit in your life, praying for the things you know not how.

God is not under any obligation to give any person something that contradicts His will. If by reason of persistence or self-effort we get something that isn't God's will for our lives, the end is always destructive. Don't push God to give you something He doesn't desire for you. You won't like it when you eventually have it. Think about Israel when they desperately sought God for a king, against God's will. God gave them what they asked, and the result was catastrophic.

I encourage you to seek God's will for every area of your life and send a save my soul (SMS) in any area needed. God's word assures us God will respond right on time. God is never late. James says, "You do not have because you do not ask" (James 4:2) then adds: "you ask and do not receive, because you ask amiss..." To ask "amiss" means to ask outside of God's will. God is not under any obligation to provide anything not in agreement with His will because when we ask for things outside of God's will, it is often to "...spend it on your pleasures"(James 4:3). This doesn't mean God isn't interested in the tiniest detail of your life, or that He's not concerned with your joy. Instead, God isn't interested in encouraging a selfish heart. He promises that when we delight ourselves in Him first, we will have our hearts' desires fulfilled (Psalm 37:4)

Things in God's will we can know for certain:
- It is God's will for you to be saved, (1 Timothy 2:4, John 3:16)
- It is God's will for you to live a righteous and holy life, (1 Thessalonians 4:3,7; Titus 2:11-12, 1 Peter 1:15-16)
- It is God's will for you to prosper and be in divine health and receive healings (both physical and emotional) (Isaiah 53, Matthew 8:16-17, 1 Peter 2:24, 3 John 1:2)
- It is God's will for you to be married and enjoy family life (1Corinthians 7:2; Psalms 68:6)

Pray with Humility

"Humble yourselves before the Lord, and He will lift you up in honor" (James 4:10).

"But God gives us more grace. That is why Scripture says: 'God opposes the proud but shows favor to the humble'" (James 4:6).

The world says, "God help those who help themselves," but the reality in the Kingdom is, God helps those who cannot help themselves. God helps the helpless, the wounded, and the broken in times of great distress if they cry out to Him. The proud do not seek help. They toil and work without calling upon the Lord. Psalm 107 uses four categories of people to illustrate God's love and mercy to all mankind. These were sets of people who cried out to God only after they have become helpless, wounded and broken. However, God in His amazing grace delivered them from the distress. The first group is listed in verses 2-7. They were the destitute (those who hunger and thirst and wander about), verses 10-14 were the second group. They were the captives (who rebel against God's Word and disdain his counsel). Verses 17-20 contain the third group. These were the sick (who transgress against God); while verses 23-28 held the fourth group who were the seamen (priding themselves in intelligence and wit).

This Psalm teaches a lot of lessons, but the one I'd like you to learn is God won't come rushing to help us until we humbly cry out to Him asking for help. In other words, until our pride is broken, God won't come to our rescue. That's exactly what happened to those four groups of people mentioned above. Isaiah says: "Our holy God lives forever in the highest heaven, and this is what he says: Though I live high above in the holy place, I am here to help those who are humble and depend only on me" (Isaiah 57:15 CEV).

In other words, God will dwell with and restore those who are humble and brokenhearted. Sometimes they are brokenhearted as a result of their own sinfulness. Sometimes they are suffering despair from the enemy's oppression. Yet, no matter the cause of their brokenhearted, God promises to help and restore them when they call on Him. We cannot fight or pray in pride. We must be willing to be humble and take our battles straight to the Lord the moment they surface. We need to have no fear about telling God how the situation is affecting or hurting you. Be real and honest with yourself and God. After all, He is your Helper. God is always waiting to help you.

BE PERSISTENT WHEN YOU PRAY

"Pray without ceasing." 1 Thessalonians 5:17

In Luke 18:1-8, Jesus gave a parable starting with these words, "men always ought to pray and not lose heart (give up)." It was a parable about a widow in a certain city whose judge didn't fear God. The judge also had no regard for man. This widow came to the judge with one request, "Give me justice from my enemy." The judge was adamant against doing anything for the widow for a while, but that didn't break the widow's morale. Instead, every day, day in and day out, she continued asking the judge for her same request, "Give me justice from my enemy." When it became obvious to the judge this woman wouldn't relent, the wicked judge said: "And for a time he would not; but later he said to himself, though I have neither reverence or fear for God nor respect or consideration for man, Yet because this widow continues to bother me, I will defend and protect and avenge her, lest she give me intolerable annoyance and wear me out by her continual coming or at the last she come and rail on me or assault me or strangle me" (Luke 18:4 – 5 AMP).

Notice the judge's reasons for giving the widow her request was because she troubled him continually. She gave him no rest. She wouldn't give up. The widow's determination was the positive affirmation Jesus used to encourage Believers, "men always ought to pray and not give up." Does this describe your attitude in prayer? This kind of persistent attitude in prayer is a sign of faithfulness that pleases and honors the Lord. Jesus continued: "Then the Lord said, Hear what the unjust judge said. And shall God not avenge His own elect who cry out day and night to Him, though He bears long with them? I tell you that He will defend and protect them speedily. However, when the Son of Man comes, will He find [persistence in faith on the earth]?" (Luke 18:6-8).

In other words, Jesus was saying compare the wicked judge, the Heavenly Father is full of compassion and love. If a wicked judge can give what is good and right to the widow, what do you think the God of love, a kind and faithful Judge will do? Jesus' final question in this passage implies if God's people didn't have their petitions, it wasn't God's fault. Any fault would be with the ones who weren't persistent in faith like this widow. I want you to remember nobody who ever came to Jesus seeking help during His earthly ministry ever went away without the help they needed. Recall blind Bartimaeus. He cried out to Jesus for mercy, even when people around him told him to shut up and discouraged him. Bartimaeus didn't back down; rather he cried out even more. To his cries, Jesus responded with mercy and grace.

You recall my friend whom I shared her story in the introduction? Well, what I didn't say there is how Lily and I prayed for her virtually every week for the three years for her Mr. Right to come. We had her name in our yearly prayer cards and held many all-night prayers where we reminded God about her marriage again and again. Even when the date for the wedding was fixed, we never stopped praying. We prayed until the marriage became a reality. Lily and I learnt this system of prayer from Isaiah 62:6-7. The scripture says "Do not keep silent and give Him (God) no rest till He (God) establish you and make your life an attraction of praise and beauty."

I encourage you when you ask God for what is His will for you, pray until you have it. Don't back down no matter what or who gives you a push back. The man of God, Robert H. Schuller, once said, "God's delay is not God's denial." Pray steadfastly until your request becomes reality.

Pray with Praise

"Do not be anxious about anything, but in every situation, by prayer and petition, with thanksgiving, present your requests to God." Philippians 4:6

The Apostle Paul encourages Believers to pray with thanksgiving. Thanksgiving is a form of praise. With prayer we invite God but through praise God comes down with His presence and power covering us. The reason is because praise is pleasing and beautiful to God (see Psalm 147:1). In other words, praise attracts God's attention similar to the way we are attracted to something we love and desire. God loves and desires our praise not just our prayers.

For instance, when Paul and Silas were jailed in Philippi because they delivered a young woman from a demonic spirit that her masters were using to make money. These faithful men didn't become worried, upset or disturbed. Instead, the Bible tells us at midnight Paul and Silas in jail prayed and sang praises unto God. The prisoners around heard them. ***Suddenly***, God's empowering presence and power reached down in the form of a great earthquake, and the foundations of the prison were shaken. All the doors opened, and everyone's chains were loosed (See Acts 16:16–26).

Similarly, the power of pure praise will free you from any bondage. When you pray and praise God, His empowering presence and power comes down suddenly and breaks off whatever is holding you back from going forward in life. If you want to enter into a season of "suddenly" I encourage you to start praying and singing praises of thanksgiving unto God. Give thanks to the Lord for all the things He has done. Offer Him praise with your prayers until your petitions become reality.

Rest, Wait, and See

To *"rest"* means to *"cease from your work;"* while to *"wait"* means *"to expect your desires."* To *"see"* means *"to experience your desires."* When we put all these words together, they create the concept: *"cease from your works when you're expecting to experience your desires."* However, this of course is only after you have done your part. We are called to do nothing but "stand" when we have done all that we can do. Standing is our part. Paul exhorted the Ephesians on how to engage spiritual warfare: "Therefore take up the whole armor of God that you may be able to withstand in the evil day, and *having done all, stand*" (Ephesians 6:13).

The word "stand" means to cease from your work. After you've done all, stand and expect to experience your request soon. God has gone into work on your behalf, because your prayers have started a fight against the kingdom of darkness. You should know the enemy is no match for our God; your victory is sure. Whenever you enter into your rest, the Lord will not rest until you have the victory. Remember Psalm 121:4 tells us God doesn't sleep nor slumber. He has no need for sleep. Never is God ignorant of our pleas for help while slumbering. Instead, He is always awake, always alert, and always bringing things into order for your good.

Some years ago, when my faith was under serious attack from delay, disappointments and failure, a senior Christian friend of mine was standing with me in prayer. Then my friend said to me, *"Sometimes we are just called to stand when we can do nothing else."* She wrote those words as a reply to my previous message where I sounded like I had done everything godly I knew to do. Here is what I want you to know, I held on to those encouraging words even though it wasn't easy, then the Lord helped me through the process.

All I can remember now is that my trials didn't last forever, and my miracles arrived at the right time. Now I'm sharing those same words with you, and I want you to hold on to them. I now have new struggles, different from those in the past. I'm glad for them too; I have more experience now and know God has been faithful in the past and will be faithful in the future. Thankfully, this is exactly what delay, disappointment and failure is building in you too.

Rest, wait and see what the Lord will do in your life. David charged us with the same thing in Psalm 37:7, he says, *"Rest in the Lord, and wait patiently for Him."* However, to stand (Rest, Wait and See) is still not a passive season, even though it's not an aggressive one either. It's a time of hope, trust, and thanksgiving. In Romans 4:20, the Bible tells us Abraham irrespective of his plight didn't waver at the promise of God through unbelief, but was strengthened in faith, giving glory to God. You can see the elements of hope, trust and thanksgiving in Abraham's attitude. That's exactly what God expects from us after we have done all. Let me tell you, if you can thank God in crisis, you've touched the heart of God. Thanking God in crisis and heartache is the highest form of thanksgiving.

7 Irresistible Prayers

1. Stand In Righteousness

2. Pray with Expectation & Faith

3. Be Specific

4. Ask According to God's Will

5. Pray with Humility

6. Be Persistent

7. Pray with Praise

CHAPTER 12

GOD'S PAY DAY

*"Blessed is the man who endures temptation;
for when he has been approved, he will receive the
crown of life which the Lord has promised to those
who love Him."*
James 1:12

God has a remembrance day for each of us. This is the day God rewards our faith, patience, and good works. However, when I talk about God's Remembrance Day, it doesn't mean God forgot you at any other time. No. God Himself promised He will never forget you. He has inscribed your name in the palms of His hands. You are continually before Him (see Isaiah 49:14-16). Rather, it means God has a right time for everything to happen in life.

God's pay day is like a worker's pay day, where workers receive wage or salary for their services. This pay or salary fulfills twofold purpose: First, pay serves as a relief. *Longman Dictionary of Contemporary English* defines "relief" as a "feeling of comfort when something frightening, worrying or painful has ended." It makes you really happy, excited, and joyful, because it takes away the pain, the stress, and fatigue of our labor. In other words, when a worker gets his pay, it refreshes or renews him from the stress of the labor. Secondly, a pay or salary serves as a motivation. *Longman Dictionary of Contemporary English* defines "motivation" as "the eagerness and willingness to do something without needing to be told or forced to do it." If we put both definitions together, we understand someone who was feeling really excited that the pain of waking up early and working all day, closing late has ended and is eager and willing to go through the same process. Even better, the person continues to get up and work without being told or forced to do so because he has received the reward of his pay. The power of wages or reward serves as a strong motivation. It helps us enjoy doing something even that is a burden. To put it simply, pay relieves and refreshes us for today and motivates us for tomorrow.

Conversely, without any reward, people are not eager or willing to do something or go through a process that was frightening, worrying, and painful except by force. Perhaps you can see why employers pay employees. The same is true in how God deals with His people. In short, God is the original model for our worldly system. God is the author of the pay system. He offers rewards to relief, refresh, renew and motivate His people through times of delay and discouragement. Look at these words from the prophet Isaiah: "But those who wait on the Lord shall renew their strength; they shall mount up with wings like eagles, they shall run and not be weary, they shall walk and not faint" (Isaiah 40:31).

In other words, God pays us by refreshing and renewing us from our suffering and motivates us to trust Him for greater things tomorrow. This reward from God is twofold: in this life and the age to come (Mark 10:29-30). However, in this book we aren't looking into the eternal rewards for Believers. As to the rewards on earth, God is never late, though sometimes we might feel He is. Solomon says in proverbs: "Withhold not good from those to whom it is due [its rightful owners], when it is in the power of your hand to do it. Do not say to your neighbor, Go, and come again; and tomorrow I will give it, when you have it with you" (Proverbs 3:27-28AMP).

Do you think if you're due a reward, God will deny you of your rightful pay? God forbid! That is incompatible with God's nature and ways. In fact, in the Old Testament when God gave the Israelites several laws on how to govern everything about them, one of them involves how they ought to pay their employees promptly, right on time: "The wages of him that is hired shall not abide with you all night until the morning" (Leviticus 19:13). God who gave this law is sure to model it. Why do some people appear overdue for their reward, as if God is just keeping them waiting?

WHY DOES GOD KEEP HIS PEOPLE WAITING?

C.S Lewis once said, "I am sure God Keep no one waiting. Unless He sees that it is good for them to wait."[1] God only keeps His children waiting when it's good for them to wait. If you're wondering what that might mean, let me say it another way. God only keeps His people waiting when they have not yet passed the test of patience or endurance (see James 1:12). Let me use the life of Joseph in the Bible to illustrate this truth. Joseph waited for thirteen years before God's promise to him was fulfilled. He even spent two additional years after he asked Pharaoh's butler for help. The scripture says " Yet did not the chief butler remember Joseph, but forgot him (Genesis 40:23).

Why would God allow the butler to forget Joseph? Joseph had not yet finished his season of testing. Look at what the words of the Psalmist: "Joseph remained slave until His (God) own words had come true, and the LORD had finished testing him" (Psalm 105:19 CEV). Did you see that? Joseph was under a series of tests. For him this season of testing lasted thirteen years including intense suffering and slavery. In other words, God used Joseph's thirteen years of slavery to test and prepare him for the position of power he would rule. The scripture records he was tested for purity with Potiphar's wife, and for integrity, accountability, and faithfulness as Potiphar's manager. This was ultimately a test of Joseph's patience.

Patience is the proof of love for God and other people. If we can be patient to endure, we can succeed in every temptation the enemy would ever throw at us. This was why Joseph was able to forgive his brothers despite the evil they did to him. If he had not passed the test of patience, he would've ended up behaving like the unforgiving or impatient servant discussed in Matthew chapter 18. If Joseph had cultivated a bitter or cruel heart, he would have ended up destroying God's purpose of preserving His people in Egypt until the appointed time to return to the Promised Land. The impatience of one man can wreck an entire generation.

This is why when we are facing delays, disappointments, and failures, God is using those seasons to test your patience. It is only after you have passed the test, you are qualified for your reward. It doesn't mean that God wants to see perfection before He qualifies or promotes you. No; God isn't looking for perfection from us. He is looking after the good of our heart. We need to keep our heart set on God and His kingdom. In doing so, we will be surprised what the Lord will do for us. Now let us dive into the things we should be expecting to experience on our pay day.

---

1. Goodreads. (n.d.). A quote by C.S. Lewis. Goodreads. https://www.goodreads.com/quotes/8146709-the-hall-is-a-place-to-wait-in-a-place.

DOORS WILL OPEN ON THEIR OWN

In the Bible, open doors symbolize opportunities. The apostle Paul often used this symbol when he talked about doors being open for him to preach the Gospel (1 Corinthians 16:9, 2 Corinthians 2:12). This is what Believers experience on God's pay day. Doors or opportunities are open wide of their own, without you knocking or doing anything to open them. It's that "suddenly" moment when you seem to get rich or famous overnight, though you've toiled for years. It's when your Mr. Right or Mrs. Right walks into your life without any notice. It's the sudden business deal or awesome job; it's your prodigal child or spouse running home. It's the "suddenly it happens" moment. Jesus told the church of Philadelphia: "I know thy works: see, I have set before you an open door, and no one can shut it: for you have a little strength, have kept My word, and have not denied My name" (Revelation 3:8).

This means no man, demon, or other enemy is able to close the doors God opens. The doors will open at God's time after you have proved your patience. These doors could even be doors you have knocked on before when they didn't open. Remember Joseph had previously asked the butler of Pharaoh for help. He knocked on the door to his freedom, the timing wasn't right and the butler forgot him (see Genesis 40:14, 23). But when Joseph's pay day came, hear what the butler himself said to Pharaoh: "Then the chief butler spoke to Pharaoh, saying, I remember my faults this day: When Pharaoh was angry with his servants, and put me in custody in the house of the captain of the guard, both me and the chief baker: we each had a dream in one night, he and I. Each of us dreamed according to the interpretation of his own dream. Now there was a young Hebrew man with us there, a servant to the captain of the guard; and we told him, and he interpreted our dreams for us; to each man he interpreted according to his own dream. And it came to pass, just as he interpreted for us, so it happened. He restored me to my office, and he hanged him" (Genesis 41:9-13).

Notice when God remembered Joseph, the butler who had forgotten him before remembered Joseph. This means when God remembers you, men will remember you too. Do not fret because people are rejecting you, or those you've once helped have forgotten you. Do not be alarmed when the doors you're knocking are not opening. Instead, be patient and allow God to turn things around on their own accord. Then just like Joseph, your disappointments will become divine appointments.

God's Fast Lane

God can change any situation in a split second. In fact, God will change your situation when you wait patiently for Him. On your pay day, God will put you into His fast lane. In God's fast lane, things start happening faster than you could imagine. Things will happen suddenly, in a twinkling of an eye. It's like after so much darkness, in a moment of light or in a split second, God's promises suddenly become reality. You won't be able to explain the rate at which positive things are happening. In fact, you'll be baffled and confused, but filled with joy. At this time, you will look for worries, anxieties, fears, sorrows and discouragement, but you won't find them anymore. They have been defeated and are gone. There is great joy, excitement, and peace to fill your heart in your new season—your season of acceleration.

When God puts you in His fast lane, it means you are in your season of acceleration. In this season, things will happen more and more quickly than you expected. Such that when you look back, you never see any time was actually lost, because God Himself has redeems the time. This was the story of Joseph when Pharaoh commanded that he be brought out of prison immediately: "Then Pharaoh sent and called Joseph, and they brought him quickly out of the dungeon; and he shaved, changed his clothing, and came to Pharaoh" (Genesis 41:14).

Overnight! Without any delay Joseph became the second most powerful person in Egypt. If Joseph had been a public servant or politician, it would have taken him a lifetime of experience and service before he could attain this height, if ever. These kinds of exultations are only possible through the power of God. Recall the section, *"7 Lies We Can't Believe."* God can do for you in one day what would take a human a thousand years to achieve. That's divine speed!

That is exactly what happened to Lily and I months after our wedding. Lily and I got married and had no furniture or electronics in our house. All we had was a single mattress on the floor, our clothes, bags, and kitchen utensils. The monthly support one of our Christian friends gave to us was not enough to afford any furniture or electronics unless we wanted to starve. But, even then, it would take us years to have the money for furniture and electronics. Yet, we continued to pray, trusting God for furniture and electronics. A couple of times, we even visited showrooms though when we had no money. We were walking in faith. Eventually, Lily became pregnant with our daughter, and we became more serious in our prayers. Newborns attract families and friends. Then one day, precisely two months before the birth, one of our partners said the Lord put in her heart to give us a certain amount of money for furniture and electronics. WOW!

We'd never told her of our need, only prayed and let God work. To God be the glory, the cash was wired to us. When we converted the money into Nigeria naira, it was exactly enough to pay for the furniture and electronics we needed for our house. In one day, suddenly we had furniture and electronics. When friends who visited our house the previous week or a day before came visiting again, they were in awe of the beauty of our home. The fact is, they couldn't hide their shock or feelings. I have seen God's faithfulness in action. I want to encourage you with our story. Relax and wait for God. He will launch you into your destiny suddenly. Your overnight success will shock your mockers and maybe even a little of yourself.

THE GLORY WILL DWARF THE SUFFERING

According to *Bridgeway Bible Dictionary* the word "glory" when used by people or things in relation to everyday life indicates nothing more than "honor, fame, power, wealth or splendor." In comparison, "suffering" means "the hardship or pain we undergo." The term "dwarf" simply means "to lessen; to make or keep small." Putting all these definitions together, we have: ***"the honor, fame, power, wealth or splendor that is coming will make your present hardship or pain too small."*** The pain will become so small you will lose remembrance of it. Your present hardship will be a distant memory because of the glory God was rewarding you with. Hear what Paul wrote to believers in Rome: "For I consider that the sufferings of this present time are not worthy to be compared with the glory which shall be revealed in us" (Romans 8:18). I love The Message Bible rendition of this scripture: "That's why I don't think there's any comparison between the present hard times and the coming good times" (MSG).

The Holy Spirit is saying right now good times are coming for you that will make you forget your present hard times. Thank you, Jesus! Maybe you're thinking is that possible? How could you ever forget the pains you're going through? With God, all things are possible. Allow me to take you back to Joseph's story. After Pharaoh made Joseph the governor of Egypt, the Bible said he also gave Joseph a wife: "and he gave him as a wife Asenath, the daughter of Poti-Pherah priest of On…" (Genesis 41:45). In verse 50, Asenath bore two sons to Joseph. Look at the names chosen for Joseph's first born son: "Joseph called the name of the firstborn Manasseh: *"For God has made me forget all my toil and all my father's house"* (Genesis 41:51).

Joseph states he lost remembrance of the thirteen years of his hardship and the betrayal and disappointments his brothers caused him. It's as if they were deleted from his memory. Listen to what Joseph told his brothers to tell his father when he was inviting Jacob and his entire household to come and dwell in Goshen safely: *"So you shall tell my father of all my glory* in Egypt, and of all that you have seen; and you shall hurry and bring my father down here" (Genesis 45:13).

Did you notice I highlighted the phrase "all my glory?" Joseph was referring to his honor, fame, power, wealth and splendor in Egypt. These were so great, they outweighed every suffering he had ever experienced in his lifetime. This is how God will reward you. He will give you so much to enjoy that you will never have time to remember your previous suffering or tough times. Jesus confirms this truth when He encouraged the disciples before His death. He used the illustration of a woman in childbirth: before, during and after labor to illustrate how His disciples will feel because of His suffering, death and resurrection: "Most assuredly, I say to you, that you will weep and lament, but the world will rejoice: and you will be sorrowful, **but your sorrow will be turned into joy.** *A woman, when she is in labor, has sorrow, because her hour has come: but as soon as she has given birth to the child, she no longer remembers the anguish, for joy that a human being has been born into the world"* (John 16:20-21).

What a comforting promise! In other words, **your sorrow will only last for a short while,** but as soon as you have your reward (your baby or miracle), **the joy will replace the previous sorrow.** So be patient, pass the test. The glory and the joy are worth it.

JUSTICE FOR YOUR ENEMIES

Next issue in God's payday is for God to deal with your adversaries. The righteous and just judge of the universe will serve justice to all those who wanted you dead, joyed in your downfall, plotted evil against you, and/or the people who hurt you unjustly. What does it mean when God serves justice to your enemies? He gives them the punishment they deserve. God fights against your enemy, fighting for you. He frustrates and renders your enemies powerless. Instead of you, your enemies become the victims of the evil they once poured out on you. You become the victor. See what the LORD did to Pharaoh and all the host of Egypt in the Red Sea after the Israelites were mistreated and fled Egypt. God fought for Israel. Hear Moses words: "The Lord will fight for you, and you shall hold your peace…so the children of Israel went into the midst of the sea on the dry ground, and the water were a wall to them on their right hand and on their left and Moses stretched out his hand over the sea; and when the morning appeared, the sea returned to its full depth, while the Egyptians were fleeing into it. So the Lord overthrew the Egyptians in the midst of the sea" (Exodus 14:14, 22, 27). The Lord consumed the Egyptians as He promised Abraham previously (see Genesis 15:13-14). We cannot take justice into our own hands and must allow God to deal with our enemies. Our battles belong to the Lord.

Another example in the Bible of God dealing with injustice is found in the Book of Esther. Haman, a wicked man, plotted to destroy Mordecai and the Jews, but God fought for His people. Not only did God bless Israel, but He gave Haman the punishment He deserved. Haman's wicked plan caused Queen Esther to declare three days of prayers and fasting for the Jewish people in all the King's provinces. As they cried out to God, God responded to free them. The gallows Haman and his conspirators had built for Mordecai to be hanged became the instrument of his own death: "Now Harbonah, one of the eunuchs, said to the king, 'Look! The gallows, fifty cubits high, which Haman made for Mordecai, who spoke good on the king's behalf, is standing at the house of Haman.' Then the king said, 'Hang him on it.' So they hanged Haman on the gallows that he had prepared for Mordecai. Then was the king's wrath subsided" (Esther 7:9-10).

Let the Bible give you confidence about God's justice system. It's an honest and fair system. We need not fear evil doers or oppressors. God will reward them with their own evil. Look at the words of David when Saul was after his life: *"He (God) will repay my enemies for their evil"* (Psalms 54:5). Indeed, God paid Saul for his wickedness against David, with Saul's own death and the destruction of his kingdom.

As part of His glory, God repays our enemies for their evil. Even our real enemy, Satan and his demons, won't escape God's punishment for all the evil they have caused God's children. This is why John the apostle tells Believers God will serve eternal justice to the devil in the lake of fire: "The devil, who deceived them, was cast into the lake of fire and brimstone where the beast and the false prophet are. And they will be tormented day and night forever and ever" (Revelation 20:10).

GOD WILL GIVE YOU A NEW SONG

Last but not the least, God will give you a new song when you wait for His right time. A new song is your success story, something that keeps people who hear it in awe of God. Also, a new song is a praise of God springing out of your heart and spirit, because your test is now a testimony. Your mess has become a message. Lily and I have many moments like this in our life and ministry. To God be the glory, some of our new songs (testimonies and message) are in this book to minister His love and care to everyone who reads this book. Most importantly, you are next in line for a new song, because God wants to use your testimonies and messages to recharge the hope and faith of people just like you in the world. Look at one of the psalms of David: "I waited patiently for the Lord; and he inclined to me, and heard my cry. He also brought me up out of a horrible pit, out of the miry clay, and set my feet upon a rock, and established my steps. He has put a new song in my mouth—Praise to our God; many will see it and fear, and will trust in the Lord" (Psalm 40:1-3).

Notice as David waited patiently for the Lord, the result was amazing. First, the Lord heard his cry. Next, God brought him out of his horrible situation. Then, God gave him a new song (praise of testimony) to proclaim to everyone who will hear. Cease from your work and wait to see God's goodness and faithfulness come into action to bring an end to your trials and suffering. Fret not. Hang on and don't be troubled, because your miracle is nearer than you think.

EPILOUGE

PEOPLE JUST LIKE YOU

I felt the real author of this book, the Holy Spirit, wanted me to include this as a concluding note to comfort and challenge you. First, the Lord wants you to know that you are not the only Christian in the world presently waiting to get married, have kids, start a business, start a ministry, start a career, own a house, or whatever your heart's desire. You are not the only one facing delays, disappointments, and failures. Countless Christians all over the world are suffering and waiting too. Look at the words of the apostle Peter as he comforts early Christians facing persecution for their faith under the Roman Empire: "…knowing that the same sufferings are experienced by your brotherhood in the world" (1 Peter 5:9).

The apostle encourages us to remember the same suffering (delays, disappointments and failures) we are experiencing are also being experienced by fellow Christians all over the world. Perhaps that knowledge doesn't seem comforting, but it should. One of the most difficult parts of delay, disappointment, and failure is the feeling of being alone, being forgotten. You are not alone or ever forgotten. When people realize they are not the only ones facing a particular trouble, there is often a sense of relief to their souls. Sometime ago, a friend of mine became so anxious and worried because she hasn't got a certain miracle she'd been trusting the Lord for. Later when she learned from her mother I was also trusting God for a similar kind of miracle, she responded by saying, "At last, I am not the only one going through this. Welcome to the Club, Lawrence!" My friend was comforted and encouraged, because she wasn't alone in her suffering. I believe that is exactly one of the reasons the apostle Peter wrote to the early Christians in all five provinces of Asia Minor that their sufferings were not peculiar to them alone. Christians, just like you, all over the world are suffering the same thing. You are going to come out of this delay, disappointment, or failure victoriously. We all will. Trust the Lord!

However, before Peter wrote those comforting words to the early

Christians, he first challenged them with these words, "Resist him (the devil) steadfast in faith." This means we don't just sit and do nothing while waiting. Instead, we allow God's Spirit in us to rise up to challenge, fight, withstand and oppose the devil with God's word and prayers in faith. This is the attitude giving victory to countless Christians all over the world. This is the attitude that will make you an overcomer.

Words that comfort and encourage us are great, but the words that challenge us are the ones that bring victory. If Christians like you everywhere are overcoming their delays, disappointments and failures, then you can too, because you have the same grace and Spirit that is indwelling in all of us as Christians. We have the same authority over the enemy because Jesus gave it to us when He died on the cross and resurrected. We may not be using our authority as we should, we might be in impatience, but God is challenging us today.

Believers in the Bible overcame their trials by faith and you can too. In fact, Jesus' statement in Matthew 11:11 meant we (New Testament Believers) who are born from above (God's kingdom) are greater than the Old Testament Saints, who overcame by faith. Starting from John the Baptist down to Daniel, Moses, Joseph, or Abraham, we are greater in power and authority than they. That's because Jesus and the Father now live inside us through the Holy Spirit. The entire Godhead that dwelt in Jesus bodily, now dwells in us. Think about that for a moment. When you remember Who lives inside of you, you'll understand that the fullness of God in you cannot fail or give up. You can fight this fight with Him, and you can win this battle.

Therefore, don't give up. Don't surrender to the enemy. Don't surrender to other people's opinion. Don't surrender to your weaknesses either. If you must surrender, surrender to the authority of God's word. Jesus is interceding for you. I'm confident as long as you hang onto God, you will never be put to shame. Get ready to celebrate your victory!

ABOUT THE AUTHOR

Lawrence E. Mukoro is a pastor, educator and author. Presently, he is the founder and pastor of Millennium Christian Church in Nigeria. His desire is to minister Christ to Africa and the world through bold and accurate teachings of God's word, adding value to people and helping them become more like Christ.

Pastor Mukoro's love for children and young people is central to his ministry. This led him and his wife, Lily, to found Millennium Christian School, a Christ-centered Nursery and Primary School where educating the complete child is their goal. The couple also serve as educators in the school. Lawrence and Lily Mukoro live in Delta, Nigeria.

Pastor Mukoro's first book, **10 Effective Ways to Children's Ministry**, was released in 2019. Detailing ten methods to easily teach Biblical truths and principles to children, **10 Effective Ways to Children's Ministry** is a must read for anyone actively leading or desiring to work in children's ministry, serving as a teacher or a daycare worker, a parent of a child, or those who have a passion to help children. This book reveals new strategies to apply proven grace-filled principles to the lives of the children you serve.

PRAYER OF SALVATION

Lord Jesus, I come to you and confess I am a sinner desperate for the salvation you offer. I believe you were sent by the Father and came to the Earth as prophesized in the scriptures and led a sinless life. You were crucified on the cross, bearing my sin, and was buried three days in the grave. Then you rose from the dead, were seen by many people before ascending into Heaven, and live forever more as my lord and savior. Thank you, Jesus, for all that you have done for me. Thank you for taking away my sin and giving me your righteousness. Thank you for sending the Holy Spirit to be with me and in me. Lord Jesus, from this day forward, I commit my life to walk in your love.

LAWRENCE MUKORO MINISTRIES

If you would like to join Lawrence Mukoro Ministries as a partner supporting children's education in Nigeria through prayer or financial resources, or if you need additional encouragement or prayer, please contact Pastor Lawrence at the address below:

Lawrence Mukoro Ministries
3, Old Warri Road, Orerokpe
Delta State, Nigeria

Telephone: +234-8136105920
Email: lawrence.mukoro@yahoo.com

Thank you for reading

Faith Under Attack
by Lawrence Mukoro

Check out our other books at

www.relevantpublishers.com

www.ingramcontent.com/pod-product-compliance
Lightning Source LLC
Chambersburg PA
CBHW071452070526
44578CB00001B/314